A Happy Miez Book

No Love for the Litter Box?

Understanding and curing house-soiling in cats

Christine Hauschild

Bibliographic information of the German National Library:
The German National Library registers this publication in the German National Bibliography;
detailed bibliographic data is available on the internet website http://dnb.d-nb.de.

No Love for the Litter Box?

Understanding and curing house-soiling in cats

© 2010 Christine Hauschild

Copyright of original edition 'Stille Örtchen für Stubentiger' © 2009 Christine Hauschild, published by Books on Demand, Norderstedt, Germany.

Artwork: Gerrit Busch

Cover art: Christine Hauschild

Layout: Christine Hauschild

Translation: Bettina von Stockfleth, C2C Media

Published and printed: Books on Demand GmbH, Norderstedt, Germany.

ISBN 9783842332966

Heartfelt thanks to Katharine Karesa for proofreading this book.

About the Author

Cat behavior therapist Christine Hauschild helps cat owners to gain a better understanding of their cats and offers strategies for curing behavioral problems and abnormal behavior. Besides all aspects of house-soiling, the most common issues she deals with are aggression against humans or cats of the same household, demonstrative vocalization, overgrooming, excessive scratch marking and anxieties. Christine Hauschild regularly conducts seminars for cat owners, covering a wide  range of topics, such as exciting entertainment for kitties, responsible cat ownership, strategies against inappropriate elimination and clicker training. The latter is also covered in her second book, *Trick Training for Cats - Smart Fun with the Clicker*, which will be published in spring 2011.

Christine Hauschild lives in Hamburg (Germany) with her two cats Eazy and ZsaZsi.

Visit her homepage at: http://www.mobile-katzenschule.de/english

Contents

Contents

In my case studies, I use many cat names I learned from friends and acquaintances, but also from clients. With the exception of litter throwing champion Easy, none of these cats have done or experienced what is described in this book. However, all stories told from the cats' perspective have happened to one of their fellow felines in exactly the manner depicted here.

Preface

Some time ago, I received a phone call from a lady living in one of the better neighborhoods in town. She asked me for help, telling me about her male cat Jocky, who she had taken in a year before as a sick stray. Ever since, Jocky had lived with her and her other cat Gina. No deep friendship had developed between Gina and Jocky. They merely tolerated each other with the odd dispute, and their owner had probably worried for some time about the not-so-happy relationship between the two cats.

Now she claimed not to know what to do. She said Jocky had begun to soil the house, which was the last straw for her. No one among her friends wanted to take him, and several veterinarians she had consulted had refused to euthanize him. When I probed her about how bad this house soiling actually was, I was shocked. Jocky had suffered from diarrhea once and relieved himself on the carpet. Another time he had thrown up some grass and hair on the couch. That was all.

We made an appointment for me to visit her house, so I could examine Gina's and Jocky's relationship more closely to improve it with suitable measures. I also hoped to be able to put in a good word for little Jocky in regard to his alleged house-soiling. The appointment was canceled by his owner. She stated that a colleague had offered to adopt Jocky. I very much hope that this colleague of hers does actually exist, and that Jocky has found a new home where he can be what he is – a normal cat!

In the context of my work as a cat psychologist, I am frequently called by desperate people who tell me about their cats' inappropriate elimination problems. About thirty to forty percent of my patients fall into this category, and I am glad that most cat owners are the exact opposite of the aforementioned lady. I have great respect for the patience many people show in dealing with their cats, and for how long they put up with their "unclean" cats – if only because they don't know any methods for curing them. At the same time, these are also the cases in which I witness major misunderstandings between humans and their cats.

This book wishes to clear up these misunderstandings and show you how you can help your cat learn to use her litter box again. Even though I will mainly address cat owners whose cats do not use the litter box, you will also learn how to avoid inappropriate elimination right from the start.

Inappropriate elimination happens even in the best circles.

1. Shedding Light on an Unwanted Habit: Facts about Unclean Cats

1.1 "See what it got you!" or: What does your cat want to tell you?

Inappropriate elimination is a sensitive issue. If a cat regularly avoids her litter box and urinates and/or defecates in your apartment or house, the consequences for the owners are often far-ranging. Carpets, cushions and mattresses can no longer be used by humans and must be disposed of. A certain, distinct smell is in the air, and thus acquaintances and friends are no longer invited for fear they might be put off. Often disputes between cat owners of the same household ensue about how to deal with the cat and "the issue," but most importantly, the relationship between the cat and her owner changes. Inappropriate elimination is a very personal matter! The more personal the space and things soiled by the cat, the more personal it becomes. It is easy for us humans to draw conclusions like "I think my tom doesn't like me anymore. He always pees on my worn clothes." "My cat urinates on the bed if I come home more than two hours later than usual – I think she wants to punish me for leaving her alone!" "I do everything for my cat! Why does he still soil my apartment?! Maybe I've spoiled him too much."

> Inappropriate eliminiation is a very personal matter.

A term that is often used by cat owners (and unfortunately also by some so-called cat experts) is "protest peeing." If a cat urinates outside the litter box, it is assumed that she does so to send her human a clear message or to express discomfort. For example that she is alone for too long, that the cat food does not meet her palate or that she is jealous of another cat or another human. This list could be continued and would become quite extensive. This is the point where I always visualize a cat's thought process: So, you are feeding me rabbit in jelly instead of beef with sauce? And to top this, you dare occupying the living room for the entire evening with your noisy human friends? Well, I'll show you how I feel about this. Let me think ... how can I really punish you? Alright, got it – I'm going to pee on your bed. I am sure you'll get the message! Do you seriously think this is realistic? I don't, for the following two reasons:

Reason Number 1:

„Protest peeing" is not a plausible concept. The train of thought I just described involves quite complex and abstract considerations. First, the cat must assume that it is possible to punish her human, including her reasons for "getting back" at the owner. Second, the cat must think about what is really important to the owner (the bed). Third, how could this important item be effectively damaged (e.g. by urinating on it). This entire construct eventually results in the abstract assumption that the cat might try to communicate something which does not relate to urination at all, i.e. food and visitors. As much as I believe that cats are very intelligent animals, I wouldn't go this far.

Reason Number 2:

In my view, the protest peeing argument is too humanizing. We humans often experience thoughts of revenge or a desire to punish others if we feel treated unfairly by them. However, cats – like all other animals – do not harbor grudges. They respond directly to their environment. They do not plan and reflect about their behavior the way we humans do when we are acting consciously – which we too, actually do only in a very limited number of situations.

For all the aforementioned reasons, the concept of protest peeing, as it is understood by most pet owners, is not plausible to me. Moreover, it significantly helps to create misunderstandings between human and cat. It is based on the premise that the "unclean" cat practices inappropriate elimination on purpose, that she has an agenda and wants to retaliate for something. If such behavior should qualify merely as self-expression, why can't the cat choose another method of expressing herself? Humans who interpret their cats' inappropriate elimination in this way feel often provoked and become angry. The urine-stained carpet becomes a personal affront – and a cat who acts like that gets left alone. Loving attention and petting sessions are not exactly high on the priority list of cat owners when they feel hurt and outraged. The human-cat relationship suffers immensely.

Inappropriate elimination as a form of non-violent resistance?

But if the cat's behavior does not qualify as protest peeing, why does she do it? Why does kitty pee, of all things, always on the living room carpet? Why does Mr. Cat always relieve himself inside the shoes left in the hall whenever you forgot to store them away? Are you sure he doesn't want to tell you that you shouldn't leave out those shoes anymore?

Cats have cat reasons for inappropriate eliminiation.

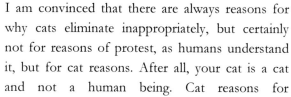

I am convinced that there are always reasons for why cats eliminate inappropriately, but certainly not for reasons of protest, as humans understand it, but for cat reasons. After all, your cat is a cat and not a human being. Cat reasons for inappropriate elimination are closely linked to a cat's well-being in her environment and to her cat-specific needs. They range from (unidentified) illnesses to the wrong place for the litter box, to stress and fear.

1.2 Punishment

Lilly tells her story:

"A couple of months ago I was going through a very rough time. My stomach hurt badly, and most painfully so when I urinated. I was constantly suffering from the urge to pee – actually, I didn't always make it to the box in time, because it hurt so much. And all of a sudden, my human became unpredictable. When he came home, he was always tense and not as friendly as before. Sometimes he would grab me and even press my head down on the floor. Once he took me by the neck, carried me into the living room, where he yelled and shook me thoroughly. Why did he do that? Why did he hurt and scare me?

Ever since this happened, I can no longer relax when he takes me in his arms. Often enough he is rather kind; he pets me and whispers things into my ear, but I am never sure he won't treat me roughly the next moment. So I have begun to wait in a safe place under the couch before I greet him. First I have to make sure that he is relaxed and in a good mood."

While cat owners will usually and generously overlook a single "accident," their cat's recurring or prolonged inappropriate elimination will sooner or later trigger strong emotions. Besides hurt feelings ("Why is she doing this to me?") and despair ("I am at the end of my rope. I don't know what to do to make her stop!"), many owners will also experience a substantial amount of anger. Personally, I can relate to this. It is more than annoying if you have to throw out the brand-new carpet or your favorite pair of shoes. It is time-consuming and expensive to replace or restore ruined wallpaper or furniture.

Nevertheless, anger is not a good advisor for how to deal with the culprit, because it often leads to punishment. Even usually loving cat owners, if they are extremely angry, will sometimes resort to archaic "educational methods," the most popular of which is to grab the cat upon discovering a urine puddle, carry her there and scold her. Some cat owners **Anger is not a good advisor.** take this procedure a step further and rub the cat's nose into the puddle or the feces. In many cases, the cat will also be carried to the site of the "mistake," where she is then verbally admonished, gets smacked on her behind or is subjected to some other form of physical punishment.

I do not wish to morally judge here. Instead, I would like to point out two entirely pragmatic reasons against punishment.

Reason Number 1:

As a rule, no kind of punishment will yield the desired result when dealing with inappropriate elimination. Your cat does not understand what you are punishing her for, i.e. what you wish to teach her. In order to allow a cat to learn through punishment, the selected method must fulfill four conditions. It must follow less than a second (!) after the cat has displayed the unwanted behavior. Second, the punishment must be dosed correctly – a too weak aversive stimulus would be ineffective, while a too strong one would cause fear, which prevents the cat from learning. Third, the punishment must follow each and every single occurrence of the unwanted behavior, plus it must be exclusively related to that behavior. We humans are rarely able to punish in such a manner that our animal will truly be able to learn something from it.

"But my cat understands exactly what's going on," I hear the protesters say. "I can tell she has peed on something because she has a guilty conscience."

Punishment does not work ...

If this scenario is familiar, you don't have a cat with a guilty conscience, but one that has keenly observed that her human is rather tense and testy. Think about it. Is it possible that upon first entering you check your entire apartment or house to see if "it" has happened again? Are you doing this in a relaxed and happy mood, or with aggravated anticipation? Then, when you have discovered a urine spot, do you look at your cat as friendly as usual? Or will your expression become fixed? Your body will tense up and your tone will change compared to other scenarios in which you talk to your cat, because you are ready to blow up. Your cat is an expert body language reader – and in such situations she reads that it is currently smarter and safer to stay away from you and look for cover. This happens not because kitty has done anything wrong, but because you are being perceived as a threat!

<u>Reason Number 2:</u>

I just stated that punishment is ineffective for curing inappropriate elimination. Nevertheless, punishing a cat does have certain effects. If you really manage to catch your cat in the act in one corner of the living room, she will avoid that particular corner in the future, but seek out another spot. This will continue to happen for as long as the real cause of her inappropriate elimination exists.

Unfortunately, punishment has the most severe impact on the cat-human relationship, especially when it involves physical assault. A single thump, shaking, or one single dipping of the cat into her urine can destroy the cat's trust in her owner permanently. If once is not enough, repeated physical violence – and this is what we are talking about here – will do.

> ... but can have serious side effects.

The visible consequences depend on the respective cat's character. However, all cats will begin to avoid their owners more often and keep their distance. Some will start to defend themselves and hiss, growl,

scratch or bite if their human approaches them in a threatening manner. Others will retreat and become very quiet – they no longer greet their human as happily as before. They will play less, cuddle less and hardly attempt to initiate any contact.

To put it bluntly: Punishment will not cure your cat's inappropriate elimination problem. Instead, you risk losing your cat's trust and destroying your special relationship with her.

The fact that punishment is not an option does not mean that you don't have alternative means of taking action. On the contrary: in the following chapters you will learn more about the (somewhat individual) toilet needs of cats. You will also learn the most common triggers of inappropriate elimination. This knowledge will

Cat-friendly and effective cures are available.

help you to provide various cat-friendly and – most importantly – effective solutions for teaching your cat to use her litter box again.

Before we proceed, we have to distinguish between two different types of inappropriate elimination.

1.3 A "typical litter box problem" or urine-marking?

When a cat begins to soil the house or apartment, we must first take a closer look at her behavior and try to figure out whether we are dealing with a "typical litter box problem" or whether the cat urine-marks. In both cases, the cat's "business" is done outside the litter box, but possibly for vastly different reasons. We will address different approaches to solving the problem.

When I talk about a "typical litter box problem," I mean that the cat defecates or urinates in the apartment or house instead of using the provided litter box which she has (in most cases) used in the past. To put it simply, the cat feels the urge to relieve herself and seeks out a new spot for this purpose – a spot that we don't find acceptable. This refusal to use the litter box is accompanied by a display of typical elimination rituals. The cat scratches and "buries" (regardless of whether there is something to dig in or not), squats and relieves herself. She then turns around to inspect her urine or feces before (imaginarily) covering it.

Litter box problem or urine-marking?

As the name already indicates, urine-marking is another process that involves urination. (It very rarely happens that an indoor cat uses feces for marking purposes.) Here we are dealing with an altogether different behavior. Compared to urination for physiological reasons, the cat's behavior and posture change. The cat approaches a certain spot, smells it, and then turns around. She flexes her spine and does a little dance with her hind feet, while the tail is erect and trembling. The standing cat then releases a spray of urine either horizontally or in an even higher arc against the place to be marked. In most cases, the sprayed spot will be sniffed before the cat walks away.

> **Urinating and urine-marking fulfill different functions.**

In addition, urine-marking has an entirely different function than physiological urinating. It is not really an elimination behavior. The cat does not urine-mark because she "needs to go to the toilet," but because she wishes to communicate something. Urine-marking is a normal means of communication among cats, besides body language and vocalization. It is usually used for territory-marking and message-posting to other cats. If a cat urine-marks indoors, this normal cat behavior is mostly triggered by specific forms of excitement. I will address this topic later.

> **Urine-marking is normal cat behavior.**

How do you know whether a cat simply pees or urine-marks, if she only does it while you are away and you cannot observe the animal's body posture? In this case, you must do some detective work and look for circumstantial evidence. Where is the urine? On horizontal or vertical surfaces? What do the chosen spots have in common? Urine-marking or spraying is generally done against vertical surfaces, preferably in corners, typically in close proximity to windows and doors, against cabinets, shoes, clothing or new items. The amount of urine is not really conclusive. Often the amount of urine is bigger when a cat regularly relieves herself, but this is not the case if certain illnesses are present. Some cats use incredible amounts of urine for marking. To complicate matters even further, some cats will even urine-mark in a squatting position, often with a trembling tail. There are also those who urinate standing, but then the site of the deed will usually give you some clues.

Since typical litter box problems and urine-marking are two different kettles of fish, they will be treated separately in the following chapters, but please don't let this lead you to believe that a cat is either "only" displaying inappropriate elimination or "only" urine-marking. If you are convinced or suspect that your cat shows both behaviors, read both chapters and follow the advice given there, please!

Some cats soil *and* urine-mark.

2. Typical Litter Box Problems

2.1 No love for the litter box?

Tom tells his story:

"When I go outside, I prefer to do my business in the flower bed next to the hedge. I like this place because I can dig deeply there without hurting my paws. At the same time, the hedge and shrubs protect me so I am rather well hidden, but I can see the two neighborhood toms approach. If this is the case, I can easily escape regardless of the direction from which they're approaching me."

What are ideal toilet conditions from a cat's point of view? This question can be answered best if we observe cats' elimination behavior outdoors, where they can freely choose the places for their business. Apparently, their decision is based on four very important criteria: surface, view, a sufficient number of locations (to move around/to escape from, if necessary) and absence of disturbances.

> **What outdoor elimination spots do cats choose?**

Surface

Normally, cats dig out a small hollow with their front paws into which they urinate or defecate. The "result" is then covered. Researchers assume that, on the one hand, covering urine and feces serves to keep the cat's own territory clean, whereas on the other hand it becomes more difficult for the feline's natural enemies to detect her. Digging is a behavior cats don't have to learn. It is instinctive and part of their normal toilet etiquette. Of course, not every surface is suitable for digging.

Typical litter box problems

Cat paw pads are equipped with innumerable nerve cells that are highly sensitive to touch. This is the reason why most cats prefer soft sand or loose soil and tend to avoid digging in hard stony ground or small pebbles. This is a behavior our domesticated cats share with their wild ancestor, the African wildcat (*Felis silvestris libyca*), who still lives in the African semi-deserts and savannahs.

View

Cats are predators, but they are also prey and have to watch out for potential attackers. They are also territorial animals who must stake out a territory and negotiate its borders as well as its shared use with other cats. When a cat roams outside, it is very important for her to detect approaching members of her kind early to avoid potential conflicts or attacks.

Cats must protect themselves from attacks.

So whenever our domesticated cats eliminate, they become extremely vulnerable for a few seconds. This is probably the reason why cats like to select spots that provide a good view in all directions, while at the same time providing some cover. Long-distance views seem to be more important than protection from being seen.

Just as important as a long-distance view are escape routes. To prevent conflicts and fights, the cat must be able to have a choice to retreat in several directions – depending on the direction from which the potential threat is approaching. If there is only a single escape route, the chosen spot will turn into a trap when the attacker decides to use it to close in!

A sufficient number of locations

A sufficient number of optional locations for elimination is crucial for two reasons. First, it is possible that the preferred spot in the flower bed left to the building is currently too dangerous, because the fierce red tom from next door is sunbathing there. An alternative on the building's other side allows the cat to relieve herself without risking a conflict or having to wait. Second, many cats do not like to deposit feces and urine in the same spot. Moreover, fresh droppings will preferably be placed away from older ones instead of "on top of them." Cats don't like to dig in their own excrements.

> **Cats like to urinate and deficate in different spots.**

Absence of disturbances

Given the choice, cats will usually look for quiet toilet locations. While doing their business, neither do they want to be threatened by strange cats, nor do they wish to be playfully ambushed by their buddy. Their place of choice will protect them from wind and rain and is a safe distance away from frightening or potentially dangerous unknown things, e.g. lawn mowers, strange people, the neighbor's dog, construction sites etc.

How do these aspects relate to indoor litter boxes?

1) Please use a litter that your cat finds pleasant. This is mostly the case for very fine-grained products. Clumping litter is more popular with owners, because it allows easier cleaning of the litter box and the cat doesn't have to dig in urine-drenched litter.

2) Covered litter boxes, particularly models with doors, are inventions by humans for humans, but certainly not anything cat experts invented for cats! Hoods block the cat's view from all directions except for the entrance area, so they cannot survey their environment. These boxes

leave only one escape route, which other cats love to block – litter box ambushing is quite popular among cats, and you will learn more about it later. To make matters worse, in no time the inside of a covered litter box begins to smell worse than the restrooms at a train station, and who wants to use those!

Do you like to use train station restrooms?

3) Your cat will be happy if you offer her several litter boxes, because they allow her to act out her natural behavior, i.e. enabling her to urinate and defecate in different places. In addition, kitty has a better chance of finding an unused or at least a less used box.

If you have a single cat, please offer her at least two litter boxes. If your household is the home of more than one cat, the number of litter boxes is even more important. To allow each cat free and unhindered access to a litter box, the following golden rule applies: The number of cats plus one is the minimum number of required litter boxes.

4) All litter boxes should be placed in such a way that the cats can relieve themselves without being disturbed. Neither human nor animal housemates should run around or make sudden noises next to the litter box, nor should hair dryers blow towards you kitty. Free access must be guaranteed at any time (and not be blocked by temporarily closed doors).

The first step is to optimize the litter box situation.

The litter boxes should be distributed in different rooms, and – if applicable – on different floors. This shortens the distances your cat has to cover and allows her to avoid other local felines.

If your cat eliminates inappropriately, the therapy always consists of two steps. Step one is optimization of the litter box situation to make it as easy as possible for your cat to return to using the litter box for elimination. To this end, we must consider *cat reasons* that will keep your cat from always using the designated box and from using it for all her business (see the following section "But why is she doing it?").

Once you made sure that your kitty has no excuses for not using a regular litter box, you may take step two. The inappropriate locations your cat has chosen as toilets (carpet, bed, corridor etc.) will be transformed into superfluous, bad, unnecessary or unacceptable alternatives (see Chapter 2.3 Solution Strategies).

2.2 "But why is she doing it?"

Illnesses and medical conditions

If a cat suddenly starts to eliminate inappropriately after she has used the offered litter boxes without any problems in the past, the first step is to find out if a medical condition is the source. There are many illnesses that can lead to inappropriate elimination. Diarrhea can have many causes, and sometimes the sick cat is unable to make it to the litter box in time. Maybe you experienced the same at some point in your life and can sympathize! Similar trouble is caused by a strong desire to urinate caused by infections of the urinary tract (FLUDT). Typically, the cat will frequently release only dribbles of urine, possibly mixed with some blood. Cats suffering from diabetes have to relieve themselves more often than healthy cats, but usually the amount of urine they release is not as small as that released by felines suffering from problems of the urinary tract and bladder. These and other illnesses are potential causes for house-soiling and must be treated.

Has your cat already seen the vet?

As soon as you notice inappropriate elimination behavior, please immediately consult a veterinarian! Often the "potty accidents" will be history as soon as your kitty is cured – unless the soiling has already turned into a habit. If this is the case, please consult the following sections.

The aforementioned illnesses directly influence the cat's elimination behavior. Moreover, there are other medical conditions that can indirectly affect your cat's elimination behavior. Painful joints and back pain can make entering and leaving the box a torturous exercise for your cat, especially if you have litter boxes with high rims. The same applies to all conditions that cause pain whenever the cat moves. In such cases, you can help your cat not only with veterinary treatment, but also by offering her a box with a low entrance. In case of extreme difficulty, you can temporarily offer your cat an old baking tray as litter box replacement. However, "temporarily" does not mean that you should ever use this tray in your kitchen again...

Old age is not an illness, but the older your cat becomes, the higher the chances she will develop illnesses and ailments, and her body will be no longer as strong as it used to be. With the increasing lifespan of indoor cats, the risk of dementia-related conditions increases as well. Like in humans, one of the symptoms can be extreme disorientation. Sometimes affected cats can no longer find their litter boxes, even though they have been in same places for years. Please be lenient toward your cat if she is suffering from dementia and help your aged kitty to be as fastidious and clean as before by placing as many litter boxes as possible in easily accessible areas and next to the carpet in the living room where your cat loves to sleep.

Make litter box access easier for old cats.

If you have ruled out illnesses as the cause of your cat's inappropriate elimination, take a critical look at your home's current "toilet situation." Some aspects that might appear insignificant from a human being's point of view can be of enormous relevance to cats!

The litter box itself

Covered or open?

Let us first make sure the litter box becomes an attractive place again. What litter box types are you currently offering your cat? Are they open or hooded? Or are they hooded and even have a door? Many cats will tolerate a covered litter box, but given the choice, they would prefer open trays. For most cats, the entrance lid is the last straw – they will look for a more comfortable litter box alternative.

Typical litter box problems

A hood on the litter box keeps the cat from surveying her environment while doing her business. She cannot see a potential threat in a timely manner, and as a consequence, your kitty will not be comfortable in such a litter box. In principle, cave-like places with small entrances can be effectively defended against attackers for a long time, but a used litter box is certainly not the best strategic spot for this purpose. The cat will be more comfortable knowing she can leave the litter box when feeling threatened.

A covered box with a door is often the last straw.

This becomes a difficult task when there is only a single escape route, namely through the small entrance opening – most likely exactly where the aggressor will sit. Thus a hooded litter box soon turns into a hooded cat trap, and who would voluntarily walk into a trap?

Covered litter boxes also make it difficult for cats to defecate properly, because usually for this purpose they squat in a more upright position than for urinating. In a covered box, kitty easily bumps her ears or head against the roof – which probably isn't very pleasant.

Cats easily bump their ears or tail in a hooded box.

"But," I hear you say, "Cherry scratches so ardently in her litter box that the litter flies left, right and center. I need a hooded litter box!" It is true that many cats leave the litter box area looking like a battlefield. In the course of a little (not too serious) competition among my friends, we found that litter throwing champion Easy occasionally manages to throw litter up to around 70 cm high (almost 28 inches). Her owner accommodated her by getting a big mortar tub with extra high walls from the local hardware store. Easy continues to have her regular power-digging workouts, but the litter stays largely where it is supposed to stay.

Another significant argument against a hooded litter box from a cat's point of view – even though this is a pro argument from the human perspective – is the fact that odors are trapped under the hood. These odors  will grow even stronger if the box has a door, cutting off fresh air supply and circulation altogether.

Many people don't wish to see their cat's feces and urine, let alone smell them. This is understandable. The same applies to cats. They, too, normally wish to see and smell as little as possible of their elimination, and they certainly don't wish to smell their companion cats' eliminations! A previously used, smelly covered litter box can prompt your cat to look for another, more agreeable elimination spot.

<u>Spring breeze?</u>

Of course, people have tried to find ways to reduce unpleasant litter box odors. Unfortunately, often the manufacturers of pet supplies cater to human needs and preferences rather than to those of cats, because the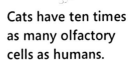

Cats have ten times as many olfactory cells as humans.

humans are buying the products. Our cats' needs are often neglected. A good example is the existence of numerous cat litters which are advertised based on their supposedly lovely fragrances. You can purchase cat litters with names like "spring breeze," "summer meadow" and many varieties of so-called "freshness" and baby powder scents. Not to mention litter box deodorizers with even more "fragrances."

Do you find that your litter has a good, but rather strong smell? We humans have about 10 to 30 million olfactory cells – our cats about 200 million. Now think about how much more intense the "fragrance" of your cat litter smells to your cat. Human beings like (or learn to like) lemony fragrances that we perceive as being "clean." Have you ever tried to get your cat to sniff a lemon or an apple? The majority of cats find the aroma of citrus fruits unappealing. Of all scents, these are the ones cats are most often exposed to in their litter boxes.

Got clumps?

Another decision regarding the litter has to be made as well: Clumping litter or non-clumping litter? Non-clumping substrates absorb the urine, which therefore remains in the box until it gets cleaned. Its grains bind the odor, so we humans don't smell much of it. But in most cases, our cats' noses cannot be fooled, and some cats will avoid their waste-filled litter boxes after a few days unless these boxes are thoroughly cleaned. Clumping litter allows you to scoop out your cat's "fresh products." Both the litter box and the remaining litter stay and smell cleaner for a longer time.

Fine-grained litter feels more pleasant under the paws.

In addition, the substrate should be as comfortable as possible for the cat's paws. Compared to wood pellets (which gather at the bottom of the box and begin to stink, while on the surface 'herbal' scents daze human and cat alike) and coarse-grained litter that is uncomfortable or painful for cats to step on and dig in, fine-grained litter is favored by the overwhelming majority of cats.

Plastic liners for the litter box?

There is another invention meant to make the lives of cat-owning folk easier. Plastic liners, which are placed under the litter so you can remove the litter in one go and be free from the obligation of cleaning the litter tray. In theory, that is. In practice, cats regularly catch their claws in the plastic film, which causes various problems. The "scratching experience" is no longer the same if kitty gets stuck on the plastic all the time. In her attempts to untangle her claws, litter is often catapulted through the air, which is unpleasant for the feline who gets hit by these miniature projectiles. Plus the claws puncture the plastic film, so the urine seeps to the bottom and gathers in the tray without being absorbed by the litter. Can you imagine the stench after a couple of days? Last but not least, the litter box must be scrubbed now anyway – or even more often! So stay away from plastic liners!

Plastic liners are a waste of money.

Dwarf or giant?

Finally you should take a good hard look at your litter boxes and ask yourself "Does my cat really fit into them?" Fitting in means: without having to squeeze herself into the box or hanging halfway over the rim. If you got your cat as a kitten, you may have purchased a litter box that is too small now. Have you noticed that your cat has grown significantly in the meantime?

Lucy tells her story:

"When I was a kitten, my litter box was okay, but lately I am having trouble using it. It has become so small. Since it stands in a corner, I cannot put my head over the rim. For this reason, it occasionally happens that something falls over the rim. This is so embarrassing, because I cannot cover it there, and its stench fills the entire room."

Many litter boxes in the market are not really big enough for an average 10 lbs. cat to comfortably turn around in while she is scratching a suitable depression for her business. A hood makes matters worse, because the cat cannot even lean over the rim. Equally problematic are corner models that look big, but their narrow corners are hardly of any use to cats.

Typical litter box problems

Please choose litter boxes that will allow your cat to turn around comfortably without having to step on or over the rim.

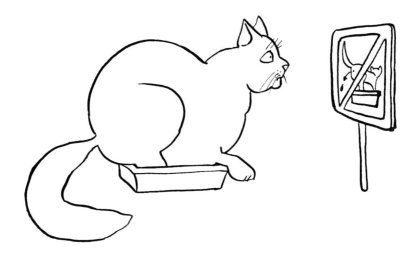

Do as you would be done by!

Mimi tells her story:

"At home, I have a litter box in the hallway. Whenever my humans let me go outside, I rather do my business outside. This combination is okay for me as long as my human cleans my box very often.

A while ago, my human left me for four days for the first time. Once a day, one of his friends came over to feed me, play with me and clean my box. However, I wasn't allowed to go out during this time, so my litter box filled up fast, and as early as on the first day around noon I began to suppress the urge to go, because my box was used and I didn't want to go in there. Fortunately, on that day the woman arrived early in the evening, so I could use the box right after it had been cleaned. On the next day, she showed up much, much later, and I didn't know what to do, so I relieved myself next to the box. I didn't want to, but there was no way I could have entered that box! The smell was so gross, and I couldn't wait any longer, so I did my business as close to the box as possible... This continued for the next two days – it was horrible! Luckily, finally my human returned, and he makes sure my litter box gets cleaned regularly."

Hygiene is very important to cats – even though you might have a very different impression because your cat soils the house. Often the very fastidious cats are the ones who begin to soil.

> **Cats dislike stepping into their own elimination.**

They hate to step into their own feces and urine, and some of them don't like to urinate in a box that already contains feces (or vice versa). How clean a litter box must be kept varies from cat to cat. If you own indoor cats who never venture outside and have no alternatives to their indoor litter boxes, you should at least scoop out the boxes in the morning and at night. Some cats refuse to use a litter box that has previously been used by themselves or another cat. If you have such a cat, then these principles are basically written in stone, and therefore it is best to remove the cat's waste as soon as you notice the box has been used. On the other hand, you should be prepared for longer absences when you are not available for personal litter box service. During such periods, your kitty must have a sufficient number of litter boxes at her disposal.

Besides the regular removal of urine clumps and feces, the entire litter must be changed periodically and the trays be washed with a neutral cleaning agent. Depending on how often

> **Compare your cat's litter box to your own toilet.**

the litter boxes are frequented, which varies due to the number of cats and if they can go outside, a thorough cleaning is recommended every fourteen days. Should you notice earlier that the boxes are badly soiled, e.g. their sides or rims, you will have to clean them before the appointed date. As a basic rule, keep the following in mind: The litter boxes should be kept so clean that *you* wouldn't mind using them.

All good litter boxes come in...

You already learned what type of litter box is most suitable for your cat; you have thought about its shape and size, and you have chosen a good litter. Moreover, you always show up on time to clean the box, but how many litter boxes do you actually need? The question itself is misleading, because people usually want to have as little to do with litter boxes as possible. They are happy to have fewer rather than more, so two cats living in the same household often have to share the same litter box.

The correct question is "How many litter boxes do your cats need?" The correct answer depends on various factors. How many cats do you have? How big is your apartment or house? Are your cats healthy? How old are your cats?

The rule of thumb for the minimum number of litter boxes is:

Number of boxes = Number of cats plus 1.

You should be so kind to offer two litter boxes even to your single cat, so that she can defecate and urinate in separate boxes, if she chooses. By separate, I mean separate. Two litter boxes placed side by side or even stacked hooded litter boxes do not qualify as two litter boxes, but as one.

At least one litter box should be placed on each floor.

If your apartment or house has more than one floor, each floor should be equipped with at least one litter box. If you own a spacious apartment or house, you should calculate one litter box for every 50-60 square meters (approx. 540-640 square feet).

These rules apply to healthy adult cats. Things look different if your kitty is very young, very old or sick. In these cases, your cat will often need a higher number of litter boxes, so she won't have to walk far to reach one of them. If your cat is old or suffering pain, taking long walks to the litter box can be too exhausting. A kitten won't make it to the next room in time if she has to relieve herself right after waking up or in the middle of an exciting game.

A good place for kitty's business?

Not only is it important to provide a sufficient number of litter boxes. Another significant aspect is the placement of single boxes. Cats and humans often have very different opinions when it comes to choosing the perfect spot for a litter box.

Typical litter box problems

Humans like boxes that are almost invisible, i.e. well hidden in far away corners, under the sink, in a den, behind doors... Often the litter box locations are determined by ruling out all the undesirable spots. *Not in the living room, definitely not in the bedroom... The kitchen – no, that would be unsanitary! Let's see... What else is available?*

Many litter boxes end up in stairwells and halls, in laundry rooms or downstairs in the basement. If it has to be the kitchen, of all places, at least the litter box must be well hidden behind the washing machine.

The first aspect that is important to cats regarding the placement of their litter boxes is easy access. Have you ever visited one of those ancient apartment buildings where the bathroom is not inside the actual apartment, but only accessible by crossing the hall? This may be acceptable in the daytime, but at night? Unless you are a very secure person, you might imagine horror scenarios about who you will meet in the dark hall or who might sneak up on you. The same applies if the bathroom is too far away from where you are staying. Friends of mine

have a two-story house with a fully developed basement. The living room is on the top floor, but the bathroom is located in the basement. Lazy person that I am, it makes me think twice or more about whether I really have to go. It's a long way and cold – their basement is always so cold! Of course I follow nature's call in the end, but it's not comfortable. So if I had an acceptable alternative...

I imagine the situation to be similar for cats, who have to overcome various obstacles before they can actually use their litter box, i.e. who have to visit a different floor, open a door, use a cat flap or crawl into a cabinet. Sure, cats can do all these things, but are they doing them gladly?

Another aspect closely connected to where the litter box is placed is safety. While a cat is doing her business, she is totally defenseless for a

Cats like to enjoy litter box privacy.

couple of seconds. For this reason, she usually appreciates a quiet place for her box. Of course, "quiet" doesn't mean "behind the seventh door at the neighbor's house," but it does also not mean underneath a sink which is being used for oral hygiene while kitty wishes to relieve herself, not in a hallway that is highly frequented by dogs, children and human family members, not next to a running dishwasher, not directly beside the apartment or house door, as this is where strangers might suddenly enter the premises. Quietness means that the cat can be sure that she will not be disturbed in her litter box.

In particular, this also includes protection from other cats in the household. Litter box ambushing is a very popular sport among cats. Such ambushes work best with covered litter boxes, because the aggressor can stalk the other cat unnoticed in order to strike as soon as the victim leaves the box. It is also great fun to jump onto a hooded box in which another cat is busy. The litter box user will become scared and can even be chased out. If this is not enough to set the cat inside running, the aggressor can at least always slap the other cat or – even better – focus fully on attacking her from above when she is about to exit the box. Open litter boxes help to prevent these activities, but some cats will try to make the most of the situation regardless of what type of box is being used.

Eddy tells his story:

"My humans have set up three litter boxes for me and my buddy Murphy. Sounds good, doesn't it? Well, the downside is that all three are outside on the balcony. Two of them are hooded, and they are stacked. The third box has no cover, and it is placed next to the others. When I am indoors and realize I have to do my business, I always have to use the cat flap to get to the balcony. I hate that flap! Of course, I'll use it if I must, but I don't like to press against it with my head, and I dislike how the flap brushes across my back. Sometimes it is also very unpleasant outside, for example if it rains or there is a storm. The balcony has a roof, but it doesn't protect me from all the raindrops. One day, I urgently had to use the litter box and – of all things – Murphy was lurking behind the cat flap. He would have attacked me if I had put my head through it (he finds that extremely funny – I don't!).

Ambushing the litter box user is a popular cat sport.

Finally, I couldn't bear this any longer! I looked for a new spot indoors and decided to use the shower basin. I have really come to like the smooth feeling under my paws, and there's plenty of room. The urine drains very nicely too. I like this place much, much better than the litter boxes outside, so the shower floor has become my new litter box!"

Such a scenario becomes even more serious if the attacks are not merely play, but rather aggression. While Mickey uses his box and hovers over the depression he has just dug, Tiger approaches; the hair on his back raised. He sits down a short distance away and stares at Mickey. For us humans, this may look more harmless then if Tiger jumped at Mickey after Tiger wiggled his behind for a while. However, from a cat's point of view, Tiger's behavior is both provocative and threatening – yet unfortunately Mickey cannot get out of harm's way that very moment...

In moments like these, escape routes are of utmost importance. If Mickey's litter box sits in a corner, maybe even next to a cabinet, there may only be one way out of the box – and this is the one way Tiger is blocking. So what else can Mickey do? He can send as many appeasement signals as possible, i.e. not stare back, avert his head and move in slow motion to avoid an attack. Other than that, he can only wait and hope that Tiger will eventually leave. Unfortunately, Tiger has all the time in the world and is not inclined to let Mickey get out of his cornered position any time soon...

Escape routes are important.

If Mickey's box were placed openly in the room or bordered by a wall or cabinet only on one side, he could escape from this precarious situation by exiting in another direction. He would probably do that in slow motion, so he wouldn't provoke an attack; or he could attempt a wild flight, hoping to be fast enough. He would still be stressed, but at least he'd be given some options.

Lotta tells her story:
"Because my friend Lisa had been dead for some time, my humans brought a male kitten home three months ago. They meant well and just wanted to give me a new companion. Unfortunately, Felix is a bully. He is always stalking and assaulting me. This happens even in the unlikeliest situations. My formerly favorite litter box is in the bathroom next to the door, which is also adjacent to the living room door. If Felix hears me scratch (and I have begun

to avoid scratching), he sneaks up and positions himself behind the living room door. On a day where he is mellow, he will attack me after I have left the litter box and am about to leave the bathroom. If he is hyper – and this is normally the case – he comes running around the corner at top speed and scares me to death while I am still inside the box. Maybe he enjoys this immensely, but I definitely don't! I have almost stopped using this litter box – with the odd exception if I can be sure that he is fast asleep. Luckily, we have another litter box that he cannot sneak up on."

For all these reasons, please have a close look at your litter boxes. Is it possible for a second cat to sneak up on the boxes? Are various escape routes available to the litter box user, or will she be trapped when she is ambushed? Are litter boxes placed in different rooms, so that a cat who is also often threatened outside the litter box is not forced to walk past a feared aggressor?

"But she can do her business outside!"

Maybe while reading this chapter you have asked yourself "Other litter boxes? Why so many? And why in several rooms? Nonsense – normally my cats go outside anyway!"

Okay. In this context I would like to note that if things were so easy, and if your cats go outside anyway to do their business there, you probably wouldn't be reading this book, would you?

Filly tells her story:

"I have lived with my humans, an older couple, for almost seven years. I was always allowed to go outside. When they had to move some time ago, they chose a house with a patio especially to accommodate me. However, the new home wasn't peaceful for very long. A big tomcat moved into the house next door, and he claimed all the gardens in front of our houses. I tried to defend my territory, but he is much bigger and more self-confident than me. He bit

me badly, and the wound became infected. The next day, he even came into our house through the cat flap, right into the heart of my territory! Given my injured leg, I could only hide, and from this moment onward this is what I continued to do, because I didn't stand a chance against this strong male.

What's a cat to do if she cannot eliminate outside?

How should I have known when he would invade my house again? The garden was no longer safe anyway – I would have been even less protected there. Thus another problem developed. In the past, I always went outside to relieve myself. Now I had to look for a new spot indoors. The carpeting in the hall was acceptable, because there the urine didn't spray up against my body and my paws stayed clean. Some time later, my humans got a litter box for me, but they placed it next to the cat flap. What if the tomcat came in again? The new litter box location was too dangerous, so I continued to use the carpet.

Then my humans began to act very strangely. After they had been following me around yelling at me for a few weeks, they suddenly grabbed me, put me into the cat carrier and brought me to this horrible place where I have spent many days and nights since that fateful day. I am sitting in a cage, and there are many other cats around me, also in cages. They are dreadfully close to me, and I cannot hide anywhere. Once a day, many strange people show up and stare into my cage.

I lost everything when all I needed was protection – and a litter box in a safe place."

As a matter of fact, many cats who can come and go to their liking prefer to eliminate outdoors. Some of them do this so consistently and reliably that their owners store away the unused litter boxes after a while. For us, this is the perfect solution, because it is comfortable. We don't have to clean up after our cats, and we don't have to deal with unpleasant smells. No litter is sent flying out of the box and gets distributed all over the house via those cute kitty paws. And even better, neither we nor our visitors have to look at litter boxes.

Sometimes this arrangement between humans and cats no longer works because kitty *must* eliminate indoors. "But she can do her business outside!" I hear owners object. "Why can't she continue to go there?" Maybe your cat would even agree in principle and prefer to use your garden. However, there are various reasons to keep your cat from using it. On top of the list are doubtlessly the neighborhood cats. Has your cat run into trouble

Things change. The outdoors is no exception.

out there lately? Has she been chased or beaten up? Has a new tomcat moved into your backyard, who now regularly sits there pretending to own everything? Chances are your cat feels that it is not safe to go outside to eliminate. Would you like to use a restroom that is freely accessible to your violent neighbor, who could knock you down any time?

A less dramatic, but still serious reason for a cat to stay indoors is lasting bad weather. Where is your kitty suppose to go, unless there is a roofed or well-protected garden patch, if constant rain has turned the flower beds into a swamp or there are snow and severe frost?

Naturally cats, just like human beings, can suppress the urge to eliminate for a certain period of time and postpone their business. Apart from the fact that this is not exactly healthy, this time period is limited. Since outdoor stressors, i.e. threatening neighborhood cats, bad weather etc., can keep your cat from venturing out for a long time, your cat needs at least one acceptable (!) "emergency" litter box inside your house. Where else should she go, after all?

If your cat happens to become ill, an indoor litter box is required. If she should suffer from diarrhea or FLUTD (Feline Lower Urinary Tract

Typical litter box problems

Disease), she doesn't stand a chance of making it from the sofa to the garden without an "accident." Other ailments might make her too weak to go a long way, or she might become more sensitive to the weather. You should also keep in mind that some older cats have difficulties climbing through the small opening of a cat flap. If your cat has to choose between a long and painful walk, possibly one involving wet and cold weather, and a short trip to the warm hallway just around the corner with perfect, urine-absorbent carpeting, it is quite obvious what she will decide to do. You can keep her from making the wrong decision by offering her a thoughtfully placed, nice litter box with low walls (to avoid painful entering and exiting) as an alternative.

The litter box of horrors

Sanuk tells his story:

"Lately, I have come to fear my litter box in the hall. In the past everything was fine, but about a month ago this started to change. All of a sudden, my backside started to hurt terribly. It was hardly bearable, a burning and biting pain! After this had happened three or four times, I stopped using that box. I am lucky because there is another box in the bathroom, and I never experienced any pain there."

Just like human beings, cats learn many things by association, and they associate both good and bad things. If I enjoy a cozy atmosphere and truly delicious food at the little Italian restaurant around the corner, I will visit that restaurant more often and always look forward to the visit. However, if I begin to suffer from an upset stomach right after a meal at said restaurant and have to spend half the night in the bathroom, this establishment has definitely seen the last of me, no matter how charmingly the waiter smiles at me whenever I walk by...

As a rule, both humans and animals learn faster from negative experiences than from positive ones, and for a good reason. If a creature does not learn to recognize a threat as such and to avoid harm, it

Cats learn by association.

might not live long enough to devour that delicious meal it's been originally focusing on. Therefore, a single negative experience can sufficiently program a creature to stay away from certain places, food items or to abstain from certain actions for a very long time.

For some cats, their litter boxes become places they start to avoid to protect themselves. This can happen (in the course of an illness) if the cat associates the litter box with an onslaught of pain while urinating or defecating. Likewise, something that scares the cat can be associated with the litter box, for example a dash of water from the shower or the onset of the washing machine's spin cycle. For some cats, the bottom line might be a piece of soap that falls down from the spinning washing machine and lands in the litter box, a visiting dog who suddenly races

Does your cat associate the litter box with pain?

towards the box, a litter box that topples over with a big bang while kitty is balancing on its rim, a gust of hot air from the blow dryer her human is using... This list could go on forever, but I think you get the idea.

Another reason cats sometimes don't perceive their litter boxes to be safe anymore is created by their owners, who try to force them to use the boxes. There are two typical scenarios:

In the first scenario, the owner wishes to teach her cat that the litter box is the right place to eliminate. To this end, the cat is grabbed more or less gently and stuffed into the box. A covered litter box may require some pushing or shoving to get the cat in, particularly if kitty disagrees and uses all fours to resist. Once inside, kitty is forced to stay in the box for some time – after all, she is supposed to use the box to learn what it is for before she is allowed to exit again. This kind of torture, and we

are talking about nothing less here from the cat's point of view, has often been preceded by a first "potty accident," which the owner now tries to cure. Sometimes this method is also used to "familiarize" an adult cat or kitten with the litter box.

In the second scenario, the owner uses the limited room inside the box to trap the feline there – see the following story by Puck. This can happen for various purposes, e.g. for applying the extremely unpopular ear drops or other

> Sometimes humans turn the litter box into a dangerous place.

medication or for putting the cat directly from the litter box into the carrier. (The latter method is often used in cases where kitty not only avoids the carrier, but also the human.)

Both scenarios teach the cat something. Unfortunately, experiencing the litter box as a good and safe place for conducting some very personal business, which makes kitty extremely vulnerable, is not part of the lesson. In the worst case, a cat who does not feel safe inside the litter box will stop using it.

Puck tells his story:
"A couple of days ago, something terrible happened. I was just using my box when my human ambushed me there! I saw him coming closer, but I couldn't really move. He blocked my exit – my litter box is sitting in a corner – and grabbed me. Then he crammed something horrible tasting into my mouth and only let go of me after I had swallowed this disgusting stuff. Never again will I set a single paw into that box!"

"But in the past, she always used to...!"

In the previous chapters, I could almost hear you mutter or protest even a bit louder "But in the past, Lucky never had a problem with the covered litter box!" Your two male cats shared one litter box for the

Typical litter box problems

last five years, and it was never a problem? The litter box has always been in the basement? Your cat always used the cat flap to do her business in the litter box inside the closet? Your tomcat frequently did his business outside, even though he often got into fights with neighborhood cats? A roll of toilet paper that had accidentally fallen into the litter box once cannot be so horrifying, can it?

What counts is now.

You definitely have a point, and your objections are understandable. Maybe your cat has been clean for years; there has never been an accident, and until today the litter box situation has not changed. Yet, as a matter of fact, your kitty no longer uses the old box regularly, or maybe she has stopped using it altogether? This happens more often than you might think. Obviously some cats will reach a certain point when they will no longer tolerate urine and feces dumped in the same box, or they are no longer willing to go on a long journey to seek out a litter box that has been banished from human view. They no longer wish to balance on the rim of their box to avoid missing the litter inside the much too small tray. They are sick and tired of walking into the garden in the drizzle, or they have vowed that never again will they take the slightest risk of being hit by a flying roll of – possibly unraveling – toilet paper. Or maybe for no specific reason at all your cat has simply decided that she doesn't want to leave the room she's in to relieve herself.

We can learn from our cat's behavior.

I understand that it is an unpleasant situation for you if your cat has made up her mind to ignore the litter box, but right now there is nothing you can do but to accept this as a given. We will never know for sure what is going on inside our cats' minds, but we can learn a lot from their behavior. Imagine a cat who begins to eliminate on the living room carpet more and more often. The owners have taken their cat to the vet, who has ruled out health issues, and they have checked all the litter boxes and found nothing wrong with them – they are safe, clean, easily accessible, but there is none in the living room. They place an additional box in the living room, and from that very day onward, the cat doesn't eliminate on the carpet, but inside the box. We still don't know what is going on in this cat's mind, but we can observe that an extra litter box in the living room is obviously important to her because all of a sudden her house-soiling is history.

What I wish to say is that it doesn't help to lament about your cat's whims and wish everything was like in the good old times. If you want to eradicate your cat's inappropriate elimination, you must take the first step toward respecting your kitty's wishes and being supportive by accommodating her wishes.

You will learn more about how to compromise on terms that are acceptable both for you and your cat in the following sections.

2.3 Solution strategies for typical litter box problems

So far, we have discussed cats' needs regarding their places for elimination and what constitutes an optimal litter box situation from the cat's perspective. If you wish to help your house-soiling cat to stop this unwanted behavior, the first step is to offer her attractive litter box conditions. Once she has been given an alternative to the inappropriate spots she has become

fond of, the time for step two has come: You must convince your cat that the spots she chose are not really suitable for elimination and/or that these spots are better used for some other activity. Again, we must look at the situation from the cat's point of view.

Typical litter box problems

What smells like a litter box, is one:

This is a fact that cannot be ignored. If your cat can smell cat urine someplace, she will assume it is a legitimate spot to relieve herself again and again. Fortunately, there are effective ways to get rid of the urine odor.

However, usual household cleaners alone will not do the job, or let's say, will not do the job thoroughly enough, because they don't dissolve all of the urine's ingredients. Please stay away from any cleaning agents containing perfume, ammonia or chlorine, because they can make the problem worse.

The urine chrystals cause the penetrating smell. Begin by cleaning the soiled spot, ideally as soon as you detected it, with hot water and a neutral cleaning agent. Then put high proof alcohol on a paper towel or on an absorbent cotton ball and use it to scrub the surface. Please don't use vodka or the like, but isopropyl alcohol (40% or more) from your local drug store. Isopropyl alcohol dissolves the urine's fatty ingredients and helps to disinfect the soiled area. Finally, use a special cleaner, either an enzymatic one or one that works bacteriological to destroy the urine crystals, because the crystals are the main cause of the urine's unpleasant smell. These cleaners can be purchased at pet supply stores or on the Internet. (Since enzymatic cleaners are easier to obtain, I will only refer to these in the following text.)

Does this sound rather cumbersome to you? Well, it works and, by the way, it also works against stains caused by diarrhea! It is not only important that you can breathe in fresh air, but also that your cat can no longer smell her urine or feces.

The cleaning steps I just described are easily carried out if your kitty kindly relieved herself on a smooth surface. However, they must also be taken when carpeting, sofas or beds have been contaminated. Washable items should be soaked in enzymatic cleaner before they are put in the washing machine, where you must wash them at the highest possible temperature setting. Mattresses, sofas or big carpets that don't fit into a washing machine require hand-cleaning. It is very important to clean such items very thoroughly. If your cat's urine has seeped into the core of the mattress, alcohol and enzymatic cleaner must reach the mattress core as well. The same applies to wooden or upholstered furniture, hardwood floors, velour carpeting and even walls that have absorbed urine. Not every material will withstand such a cleaning procedure without suffering, and it is possible that your once burgundy-colored couch might end up tinted a lighter shade of red. At least you can rest assured that from now on, you'll be sitting on a thoroughly cleaned couch. Please let the cleaned areas dry completely before granting your cat access to them, because wet spots might be misunderstood as an invitation to produce new puddles there.

The right cleaning method is crucial.

In cases of extreme soiling or if cleaning the item is not feasible for other reasons, the last resort is to throw them away. This is annoying and in some cases also an expensive solution if the item has to be replaced. But please keep in mind: What smells like a litter box, is one and will continue to be one in your cat's eyes. She simply doesn't know any better.

What has been used as a litter box several times, has become one

So you have erased all traces of the incident. Very well! Unfortunately, there is some more bad news. Cats are at least as much animals of habit as we humans. Do the members of your family all have their own, customary seats at the dinner table? If so, no one will use another person's chair, right? Should this happen, it would most certainly be irritating for at least a moment. Yet sometimes we break our habits. If you redecorate your dining room and set up the dinner table and the chairs on the other side of the room, your family's long-established seating arrangement might change. However, within a short period, the new seating arrangement will become just as familiar as the old one. You don't think about it; you just use your chair.

Our cats function the same way. No matter what kind of change has occurred or what reason your kitty had for choosing a new spot to eliminate – as soon as she has used it several times, it will have become a new regular "litter box." From this moment onward, she will seek out the carpet not because the washing machine begins to spin or because the carpet already has a urine smell, but simply because the new spot on the carpet is closer and more convenient than the actual litter box.

Please do not start to scold your cat now, shoot the water pistol at her or do something else along these lines. As you have learned earlier in this book, such punishment methods can have serious side effects! Instead, you can choose between different strategies to solve your cat's house-soiling problem.

A strategic approach is better than a water pistol.

Strategy # 1: Acceptable, additional offers

Place a new, additional litter box exactly where the cat inappropriately eliminates now or in close proximity. As a rule, you should always take this step first! The point is to make it as easy as possible for your cat to behave according to your wishes. The vast majority of cats who are offered a spacious, uncovered litter box in their newly chosen elimination spot will gladly accept it and no longer eliminate outside the litter box.

You can also place litter boxes on sofas or beds, especially at times when you are not at home. These new "real" litter boxes are not supposed to stay forever, but they must be placed on the undesirable elimination spot until kitty has accepted them and learned to use them reliably. How long this will take varies. As a rule of thumb, keep in mind that if the new elimination spot has not been in use for long (i.e. less than a month), anticipate a period of about two weeks. If your cat has eliminated in this spot for a longer time, you must be prepared to leave the new litter box in place for at least a month, even if this is really inconvenient. When this period has passed and your cat uses the new box reliably, do not remove it from one day to the other. Think about where you can place it safely and conveniently for your cat and move it there gradually – inch by inch. Of course I don't mean "one inch per minute," but a maximum of six inches per day.

> **If everything else fails, put the litter box on your bed.**

Strategy # 2: Remove attractive alternatives to the box

In many cases, you can simply remove the object your cat has chosen as elimination spot. Lock the attractive peed-on rug away in a wardrobe after cleaning (until the new "real" litter box is used consistently) or throw it away, if you don't like it anymore anyway. Your cat fancies the soft cushion on your sofa as elimination spot? Simply store away the cushion for a while.

It is part of the same solution strategy to change the elimination spot your kitty chose in such a way that it will lose its attractiveness. A typical and very practical method is to cover a couch or a bed with thick plastic sheets (they must be thick enough to withstand contact with cat claws). Many cats prefer soft surfaces that absorb urine immediately and from which droplets won't splash up. Human beds fulfill these criteria. If you put a plastic sheet on your bed and your feline decides to urinate there, the bouncing droplets and little puddles pooling around her paws will be a nasty surprise for her. For many cats, using such a place is out of the question, and your bed will no longer be abused as litter box substitute.

Paws in puddles are a no-no.

Yet a little warning is in place here. Sometimes house-soiling cats develop new preferences regarding their new "litter" that must be taken seriously. They realize how pleasant it is to urinate on a carpet or on bedding – it's quiet, the fluid is absorbed immediately, nothing contaminates their paws – and end up preferring the new surface over their usual litter. This doesn't happen often, but if your cat is inclined to use the wrong litter box substitute, which has all the aforementioned qualities, you must take this into account. In such cases, do not offer your cat the new litter box filled with regular litter (which wouldn't be attractive enough to her), but put a hand towel or a cushion inside the litter box. Some cats even enjoy relieving themselves on the naked floor. If this is the case, offer an empty litter box, i.e. without any substrate inside, as an acceptable alternative to the floor.

Of course, empty litter boxes can easily be scrubbed and urine-soaked towels can be machine-washed. However, I guess it is safe to assume that you would like to return to regular litter sooner rather than later. This can be done – but please at a very slow pace! Give your cat enough time to learn. Lesson one is that the new, litter-less box is at least as attractive as your tiled floor. Once your kitty has internalized that, you may begin to fill the box with a minimal amount of litter. Start with a handful in one corner. If your kitty accepts it, add another handful the next day. If this is also okay, stick to that amount for another day and then proceed to add one more handful the day after.

> **Give your cat enough time to relearn.**

The same applies to kittens who have never learned how to use a box filled with commercially available cat litter. Some people who raise kittens at home offer them a cardboard box padded with newspaper instead (even though it still mystifies me why they would do that). With the methods I just described, such cats can learn slowly and reliably to accept the – from a human being's point of view – correct litter.

Strategy # 3: Deny access

When I tell you to make the unwanted elimination spots inaccessible to your cat, closing the doors may first come to mind. Perhaps you have done this already in the past, because it would be the most obvious approach. I kindly ask you to close doors only as a last resort, i.e. if every other method has failed – unless you live in a really big house, where one accessible room more or less doesn't make a big difference. In a regular one or two bedroom apartment in a city, reducing the living space of a cat that is not allowed to go outside is unacceptable! If there

Typical litter box problems

was a comparative of "unacceptable," I would call it even more unacceptable if you own more than one cat. They need enough space to enjoy some privacy.

Cats are extremely territorial animals. This means, among other things, that they patrol their territory on a daily basis, some of them even more often. If only a small part of their territory is suddenly cut off by a closed door and thus outside of the cat's control, this can stir up intense emotions ranging from frustration to aggression. Please think about how small our apartments and houses are compared to the territory of an outdoor cat in the country, where cats frequently venture away from their homes to cover a couple of hundred yards up to 0.6 miles. Each room that is off limits means less roaming, less activity, less external stimuli – an invitation to new behavioral problems or to the development of behavior patterns that are problematic for the cat-owning human. As things are, you are already dealing with some, so let's get back to the issue at hand.

In a small apartment, all doors must stay open.

You can make elimination spots on the floor easily inaccessible without closing doors by placing a small chest of drawers or your cat's small scratch post there. You can also move the sofa to cover the place near the wall that your kitty has been using as an elimination spot lately. If your cat likes to soil the uncovered floor, put a carpet there. Do you have a cat who enjoys doing her business in flower pots and planters? You can either cover the soil with big pebbles or obtain potted plant protectors in specialized stores. But since your cat likes the soil inside your planters so much, do her a favor: Offer her some potting soil as an easily accessible alternative in one of her litter boxes.

Strategy # 4: Change the meaning

Another strategy is to change the meaning of your cat's chosen elimination spots – that is, to give them a meaning that is incompatible with their use as litter box substitutes. This is a very cat-friendly approach, because your cat is not restricted in any way. On the contrary, she is even offered a bit more variety. The safest method is to convert the – of course meticulously cleaned – elimination spot into a feeding spot. Normally no cat will soil her feeding place, because she hates to eat in areas where she can smell litter box odors. There are two approaches you can choose. Which one will work best for you depends on your feeding routine and, naturally, on your cat's behavior.

The first approach is to convert your cat's main elimination spot into the main feeding spot, e.g. instead of feeding your cat her freshly prepared meal in the kitchen, serve it in the precarious spot in your living room from now on and do so for an extended period. Thus the new feeding place will acquire a new meaning, i.e. it will become a popular location she associates with her food. However, if your cat tends to empty her bowl fast and you feed her two or three times a day, this spot will be without food for many hours every day. In some cases, the association between living room and food will not become strong enough, and your cat might start to eliminate inappropriately again. In this case, you'll have to fall back on the second approach. Do not only feed your cat her principal meals in the former elimination spot, but additionally offer her dry food. If your cat is used to having access to dry food anyway, you will merely serve it in a new location now. If you haven't been free-feeding dry food before, start doing it (at least for a while). To prevent overeating, expose the dry food to the air for a couple of days in a cat-safe place where it will go stale. Chances are your cat won't find it appetizing enough to touch it after such treatment, yet she will recognize it as a potential meal and abstain from eliminating in its vicinity. Compared to wet food, dry food has the additional advantage that you can place it directly on the floor, the sofa or even on your bed without creating a big mess. Compared to wet food, it is much easier to use dry food to convert larger areas into feeding places.

The new meaning: A feeding place!

Like with the other strategies, you should also adhere to an elimination spot's conversion into a feeding place for several weeks. Only if your cat hasn't soiled this spot for at least a month, is it time to move the feeding place slowly, i.e. stepwise, to its original location.

As an alternative to transforming the elimination spot into a feeding place, you can also convert it into a sleeping place or kitty playground. Yet, for reasons beyond our comprehension, particularly cats' sleeping places are not always reliably kept clean, as the high number of soiled beds and sofas prove. A bit more promising are exciting playing sessions in a certain place, but since they are limited, instead of relying on these alone, I would rather recommend them as an additional strategy to be utilized with conversion of the feeding place.

In the previous sections, you have learned the most common causes of typical house-soiling problems in cats. These are illnesses and, from a cat's perspective, less than optimal litter box conditions. Then you learned a lot about different solution strategies which can be applied if the problem is recent and has occurred for acute reasons, but also if your kitty's inappropriate elimination has become chronic, i.e. a habit. In both cases, your cat must relearn what qualifies as a litter box that is acceptable to humans and felines alike. Please be aware that the longer the house-soiling has been going on, the more time you must allow for your solution strategies to work, and – most importantly – the more time you must give your cat. During her house-soiling period, your cat has learned,

> **Adhere to the changes you made for at least a month.**

for example, that the carpet is a good litter box substitute – a fact that has been established by using the carpet over a three-year period. Naturally, the retraining process, i.e. teaching the cat that from now on this very carpet is no longer a litter box, whereas the new litter box further down the hall is one, will not happen overnight!

2.4 Litter box problems as symptom of a mental disorder

Regardless of how long the house-soiling problem has existed, your cat must go through a learning process to become clean again. To be able to learn, certain prerequisites must be fulfilled. For felines, this is no different than for humans. In other words, there are circumstances that will keep a cat from learning (enough) to refrain from house-soiling. This is where we enter the realm of serious psychological problems. Don't get me wrong; I don't mean to say that inappropriate elimination isn't a serious problem. It is most certainly for the owners, but from a cat psychologist's standpoint, it does not qualify as abnormal behavior. However, it can be the symptom of a mental disorder, especially of anxieties and depression. One might say that a depressed cat feels that it is too arduous to seek out the litter box, i.e. it cannot be accomplished, while an anxious cat is unable to leave her safe hiding place to use the box. In both cases the cat has no real freedom of choice, but is a prisoner of the dark or intimidating world inside her head.

If your cat is listless over a prolonged period (more than three days) or retreats (to a place under the bed, on a wardrobe, on a shelf or the window sill) and either refuses to leave her hideaway altogether or only comes out only briefly or rarely in a crouching posture, in particular slowly or fast, if your cat shows signs of aggression when humans and/or other cats come near her, if she is attacked in her hiding place by companion cats, if her pupils dilate, her ears are flattened against the head and she tries to make herself look smaller when humans or cats approach, or if she shows a combination of these behaviors, you can be sure your feline is in great mental distress. In most cases, a depressed cat will remain

Inappropriate eliminiation is not abnormal behavior, but can be a symptom.

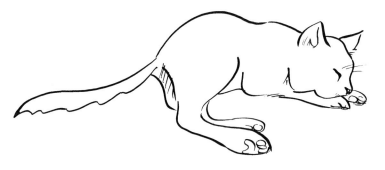

visible and won't necessarily hide, but she will remove herself from any activities, i.e. no longer participate in life. Depressed cats don't play; they eat either very little or too much, and their overall appearance is joyless.

If you suspect that your house-soiling cat is suffering from anxieties or depression, please make an appointment with your veterinarian right away to exclude physical causes of your cat's mental disorder. Depression almost always becomes manifest in the context of painful illnesses. If your cat is ailed by anxieties or no physical reason for her depression has been found, please consult a professionally trained behavior therapist. Please make sure that this person actually is really experienced (and preferably specializes) in working with cats and not with dogs!

> **Anxieties and depression require professional treatment.**

It is pivotal to your cat's quality of life – and in some cases for her survival – that the causes of her psychological problem are found and successfully addressed and/or your cat's anxieties are treated. Until this has been accomplished, please provide a litter box close to your unhappy kitty's retreat or favorite hiding place.

3. Urine-Marking

3.1 Urine-marking: A means of communication

In the previous chapters, we learned about inappropriate elimination in the classical sense, i.e. when cats don't use the litter box to do their business, but choose a spot that is unsuitable from a human's perspective instead. However, there is a second type of inappropriate elimination which has nothing to do with physiological elimination behavior. I am talking about urine-marking. When a cat urine-marks, she assumes a posture different from the one she uses for urination. After a certain spot has been sniffed, she turns her rear end toward it while standing upright. The tail is vertically raised and trembling while she scuttles in the same place, hind legs stretched, to release a spray of urine on a more or less horizontal level. The result is usually checked by sniffing before the cat is on her way again.

Spraying such marks in her territory is a normal aspect of a cat's intra-species communication, that is, her communication with other cats. As

Urine contains a lot of information.

far as we know, by sniffing these marks, cats learn which cat has been here and at approximately what time. They can also smell if unspayed cats are about to enter a fertile phase. If the animals don't know each other, these marks will at least reveal their sex. Some research indicates that cats can gather additional information about the urine-marking cat's age, health status and mood.

Unspayed cats urine-mark as part of their sexual communication, primarily when they are in heat. Unneutered males respond with excessive urine-marking, particularly in the months of the reproductive season (in most regions spring). Intact male cats also regularly urine-mark their territories outside of the reproductive season, which is why they will also do it inside the house or apartment.

Since urine-spraying is normal cat behavior, not only unneutered toms urine-mark. In most cases I encounter in the course of my work, spayed and neutered cats are the culprits. This may come as a surprise for many cat owners. Their sweet little kitty girl is supposed to urine-mark? It is quite possible, and is, as a matter of fact, anything but sweet and certainly not discreet...

Urine-marking is not just the domain of toms.

Marks are usually aimed at vertical surfaces that are on cat head level. Moreover, the chosen spot must be of strategic importance and visually distinctive. Typical marking destinations are corners near windows, door frames or doors, legs of chairs and tables, stairs and electrical outlets. Similarly attractive are items that are obviously significant for the cat, e.g. shoes and bags that carry outdoor scents, worn clothes, used towels, but also new furniture or any other type of decorative item. Maybe these things don't even have a strong scent, but one that is unfamiliar. Some of these items will lie or stand on the floor, so that the cat urine-marks downward rather than upward.

Strategically important spots are marked.

If you find puddles inside your home but fail to catch your cat in the act, the puddles' location will often allow you to draw conclusions regarding your cat's type of elimination, i.e. if you are dealing with physiological urination or urine-marking. If you find urine puddles near a wall or close to another object (couch, stereo, loudspeakers), check the vertical surfaces for traces of urine that have trickled down and pooled on the floor. If you find traces not on the floor, but on and in items, please check if these are carrying particularly enticing scents.

There has been a lot of speculation about why cats urine-mark and about what kind of mood they are in when doing it. You will often read that cats who feel insecure urine-mark, or that urine-marking cats have insecure personalities, but so far this has not been proven. As a matter of fact, many anxious and insecure felines never display marking behavior. If it is done in the presence of other cats, it is rather a sign of power and dominance. After fights, the winner will be the one who urine-marks before the eyes of the inferior cat, while the latter will cover the mark as soon as she is alone again. The same applies to scratch-marking.

Research has not yet yielded any results regarding what is going on in the minds of urine-marking cats. We know only for sure that cats will urine-mark in the very center of their territory when they are agitated. The nature of this agitation can be positive or negative, i.e. it can be triggered by events that we humans would describe as particularly pleasant, frightening, annoying or even unsettling. Fact is that cats leave their personal "calling-card" when they urine-mark, while at the same time covering strange smells (at least partially).

Whereas we "only" have to make the litter box attractive again to cure house-soiling, it is a bit more complicated to cure urine-marking. If a cat does the latter, she responds to her

> **Urine-marking is a response to the environment.**

environment and communicates in a normal, catlike manner because she has reached a certain level of agitation. Therefore, we must find out what excites the cat and try to influence the trigger(s) of her behavior, so that your cat will feel more relaxed again. This inevitably leads to the conclusion that here, too, punishment is not an option. On the contrary: if you irritate your cat with punishment, it is quite possible that her urine-marking will intensify – not as a protest, not to retaliate, but because it is a cat-specific means of expression.

Just like humans, cats are individuals who experience their environments in different ways, who respond differently to similar situations, and who are exposed to different living

> **Urine-marking is communication.**

circumstances. So it is pivotal that the search for the trigger also takes into account the cat's specific living situation. To make the search for the trigger easier, I am going to describe a couple of typical situations that are often observed in connection with urine-marking behavior in the following paragraphs. These are followed by suggestions for changing the trigger to reduce the number of urine-marking incidents and hopefully prevent them altogether.

3.2 Urine-marking triggers: Agitation due to

- Illness and/or pain

Discomfort and pain cannot only subdue an animal's behavior, they can also cause stress. Particularly feline urinary tract diseases (FLUTD), but likewise various different diseases of the central nervous system as well as painful illnesses, can be reasons for (increased) urine-marking. If your cat suddenly begins to urine-mark inside your home, please have her checked by a vet first.

- Other cats in the household

When two spayed or neutered cats live in harmony in an environment they are comfortable in, they usually communicate in a way that is unobtrusive and thus convenient for humans: body language, nose touch, gazes, vocalization, scent traces left behind with paw prints and scratching on objects. In a peaceful atmosphere, they will very rarely communicate via urine-marking. Yet the more cats live in one household, the greater the chance that at least one cat will choose this (also normal) means of expression. According to the Austrian cat behavior specialist Sabine Schroll the probability that at least one cat in a household with five cats urine-marks will rise to 75 percent. In a household with ten cats, the probability will be 100 percent.

The higher the number of cats, the higher the number of urine-marking cats.

This becomes clear immediately if you take the time to consider what it means for a cat to share her limited living space with a few or many other cats. First of all, our cats cannot decide for themselves which other cats may share their home territory. Instead we humans pick their companions with more or – unfortunately rather often – less consideration. Given adequate socialization, many cats are social animals, but this does *not* imply that a cat will automatically like every other cat who is put under her nose. A kitty we bring home because we find her funny, cute, incredibly beautiful or because she is pitiful and in need of help may be considered a true pest by the resident cat.

With the growing number of cats in the household, the number of relationships between the single cats increases as well: If you have five cats, every single cat has to manage four personal relationships with her fellows. For each relationship we have to assume that both partners do not see this relationship the same way. Instead, this relationship involves two different points of view. Moreover, each cat is affected by how the other cats get along. Have you ever lived with

Even mild tension can trigger urine-marking.

other people who are constantly arguing loudly? Or with people who will never utter a loud word while the air between them is filled with a subtle, but unbearable tension? Even if you had not been involved in their conflict, the situation will have had an effect on you. Cats feel the same way, and if you own five cats, you will already have ten different (bilateral) cat-cat relationships comprised of communication and competition, ear-licking, blocking each other's passage and sending some fur flying.

Urine-marking

It is only plausible that cats will (have to) use all means of communication at their disposal in such a complicated arrangement of relationships. Unfortunately, these means include urine-marking.

- Other animals, children or new persons

Not just other cats, but also other animal or human cohabitants can be taxing and stressful for a cat. This applies not exclusively (but especially) to those who move in and upset kitty's daily routines.

Foxi tells her story:
"Lately, my human has been visited by a male guest. This is very exciting because until now there were only the two of us. Very rarely another woman would show up, but she'd always leave after a while. It is somewhat exciting to have this man here, but I am not quite sure what to make of him yet.

Whenever he arrives in the evening and stays overnight, everything is totally different from when I am alone with my human. They will sit on the couch together, and, ooooh, I cannot really bring myself to join them. Sometimes he stirs hectically, so I prefer to keep my distance. The same goes for the bed. Usually I am sleeping at the foot of my human's bed, but that is out of the question when he is here. Who knows what might happen? And when he's in bed, his clothes are nearby, and they are so exciting! So many scents to discover, and they are so strong. I could spend hours sniffing them. After I sniffed them, I always leave some of my scent for him."

Some cats – by no means all cats! – react very sensitively to a new partner entering their owner's life. The stranger becomes a competitor for that favorite spot in bed and may ignore that Miss Kitty does not wish to be petted while perching on the sofa's armrest. What an affront that is, when *everybody else* understands that this spot means "I am here, but wish to be left alone." And this guy has such a loud and carrying voice! Also, kitty's

> **Worn clothes on the floor are an invitation to exchange scents.**

owner is constantly overlooking her – she only has eyes for him. Depending on the cat's character, such adversities can lead to frustration and/or cause insecurity. If t-shirts with the intruder's scent on them are scattered on the bedroom floor, they are an obvious invitation for the resident cat to cover the strange smell with her own scent, thus creating a more familiar atmosphere.

Dogs pose a particular challenge for cats. A new dog in the house, possibly a young one, enters the heart of the cat's territory, literally sticks his nose into her most intimate business and follows her around in his obtrusive manner while leaving his strong dog odor everywhere. Hardly any cat responds kindly to a pubescent puppy who approaches her in a happily bouncing gait, inviting her to a little romp, but some cats like to turn the tables and begin to pursue the dog that just bounced past them, seeing him as prey.

Kimmy tells her story:

"For six years – my entire life – I have lived with my humans. We were a great team. I used to sleep comfortably at the foot of their bed, and we played together a lot. Then my mistress became pregnant. I found that quite strange, because her scent changed, but I was getting used to it. After all, she continued to behave like before and played cool games with me. Then my owners began to hear many stories about cats who began to soil the house in response to a human baby. Eventually, they were so worried about this that they gave me away. I am now living at the mother's of my mistress, and I miss my humans endlessly. Life with them was wonderful and exciting. Here, I am lonely and bored out of my mind. There is not even a tree in front of the window. How could they simply pass me on? I would have been loyal to them through thick and thin!"

Babies change a cat's life fundamentally. An infant won't be as mobile as a dog for a long time and will not hassle your kitty as much as a dog. Yet in most cases a baby upsets a cat's life even more than a dog. Newborn children cause many changes on different levels. Even before the child has been born, the apartment or house will have changed. New and unfamiliar items such as a crib and a baby buggy show up, accompanied by their strange smells. Often cat owners decide that the child's room will be off limits for the cat, and all of a sudden kitty finds herself in front of a closed door – a door that cuts off an important part of her territory. Who knows what exciting or threatening things might go on in there while the door is closed?

Once the child has arrived, not only the infant's own scent is new, but also the strong smells of baby lotions, baby powder and used diapers.

The crying and screaming of small children can be unnerving to human ears – for cats with their much more sensitive hearing it can actually be torturous.

While we humans are happy about the newborn's arrival in spite of full diapers and crying, the local cat has not wished for this child. She is suddenly confronted with a strange, not exactly confidence-inspiring being in the center of her realm that brings its smells and noise, too. In addition, the behavior of her humans has changed and the cat's routine is upset: At night, kitty is driven from her favorite place between her owners' legs every couple of hours, because they have to take care of the baby. The early morning ritual of cuddling after the alarm clock beep, opening the door to the balcony and greeting the morning together, followed by a lovingly prepared and promptly served breakfast is history. Instead, now her humans often get up before the alarm clock beeps, the balcony door is neglected in favor of the door to the child's room, and breakfast is constantly postponed. In the evening, the humans' lap is always occupied by that strange new thing, and they no longer respond to invitations to play.

For some cats, the situation will become unbearable when the child enters the crawling stage and actively moves around in the cat's territory. There is hardly a child that will resist the impulse to grab a cat upon seeing her. Of course the child doesn't understand that the cat thinks she is assaulted when baby closes in on her with fast, abrupt movements and grabs her fur.

Baby begins to crawl: A tough time for your cat!

In short: Everything has changed, and from the cat's point of view, her physical integrity is no longer guaranteed. One of these two situations alone would already pose some difficulty. Combined, they pose the worst-case scenario for many cats. Please don't be too hard on your cat if she reacts according to her feline nature, i.e. tries to cover the new scents, be they baby or dog scents, with her own urine and not just by rubbing her head. Of course, this does not imply that you should do nothing when your cat starts to urine-mark in such a situation. However, it would simply be unfair to expose the cat to an extreme situation first and then part with her because she cannot adapt to the new situation right away. In Chapter 3.3, you will learn how you can help your cat in this predicament.

- Neighborhood cats

Mini tells her story:

"I have learned that some cats actually like to be very close to other cats. At the shelter, I, too, was forced to be close to others – and I hated it. Fortunately, I am my human's only cat, so I don't have to share my territory, but something that really gets to me is the calico next door. Unlike myself, she is allowed to go outside, and she frequently walks past my window. How dare she!? This is my

> **Visual contact alone can cause extreme agitation.**

window and my territory! How dare she venturing so close to me? This is the ultimate provocation. Since I cannot get outside to chase her away, I have resorted to marking the borders of my territory – the windows and the window area – to clarify who is the boss here! She might even come inside at some point. Well, she would definitely regret it!"

Not only cats trespassing into the heart of another cat's territory can upset the resident's relaxed everyday routines. Often the neighborhood cats and other visitors will cause your cat to become extremely agitated. It is not even necessary for your cat to have direct contact with the neighborhood cats, let alone get involved in hostile encounters or fights. Being able to view others through the window, sometimes even just hearing them, will be enough for some cats to feel violated. Even if your own cat never

> **Do other cats urine-mark close to your house?**

enters the garden in front of the window – as soon as the neighbor's tom shows up there, he will have your kitty's full attention, as she will sit on the window sill, possibly wildly lashing her tail.

If cats are allowed to go outside, they are forced to deal with other cats in their environment. The relationships of outdoor cats are multi-faceted and range from true friendships and polite toleration to ongoing feuds about who possesses a certain territory. In any case, your outdoor cat has to manage various situations, and not for once and all, but over and over again. Even if your cat has not engaged in any fights for months or years, there is no guarantee this will not begin to happen at some point. A new cat who has moved into the neighborhood or the death of an old feline resident can easily topple the cat community's dynamics.

Many cats will leave urine-marks outside around their home, while the house or apartment – being the center of their territory – remain unmarked. When conflicts with other neighborhood cats develop, or a strange cat enters your kitty's turf, causing her to lose her sense of security, it may become necessary for her to mark her territory more conscientiously – sometimes also indoors. This will happen particularly often if other cats urinate on the house walls or even on the cat flap. The worst-case scenario for every cat with little confidence and low social tolerance is the

Do strange cats sometimes enter your house?

brash and overbearing tom from next door actually entering the house through the cat flap or door. What if the treacherous cat owner herself has invited the supposedly cute opponent in for a snack? A disaster! Your cat's sense of security is destroyed. How will she be able to sleep well if she cannot be sure she won't be attacked the next moment?

How can she roam the house relaxed and without concern if she doesn't know who might be lurking around the next corner? What can she do if the intruder has left his appalling stench everywhere? You guessed correctly: Your cat has to spread her own scent and thus demonstrate that this is her realm!

- Hunger, impatience and happy excitement

Jumbo tells his story:

"Every day, my human is gone for a rather long time. He leaves early in the morning after hastily feeding me. At night, he comes home at different hours. If I am lucky, he returns in the late

Cats need reliable and regular feeding rituals.

afternoon, which is why I spend a lot of time in front of the window and watch out for him at that time. This is when my stomach begins to growl, too, and anyway – it's not like there is anything else to do. Unfortunately, my human never returns on time. Usually, he will arrive in the evening instead of in the afternoon. And even worse, sometimes he shows up late at night. It makes me so nervous that I cannot rely on him. I can never be sure when I will be fed again and whether I will have the opportunity to play with him today or not. The hunger makes it even more difficult for me to relax, of course. Whenever I get too tense, urine-marking in a corner of the room helps me to ease the tension a bit. Sometimes I am even so happy to see him that I have to urine-mark when he greets me."

Often joy and sorrow go hand in hand, just like agitation for positive as well as for negative reasons. Our cats are used to being fed by us humans, but this luxury also has its downside. Cats – especially indoor cats – depend on tasty and high-quality food, provided by their owners at specific feeding times. Little trouble occurs in households where food is available around the clock. Unless another feline is around who repeatedly denies access to it, the cat in residence can help herself to food anytime. However, this feeding method is not always feasible or desirable. Wet or raw food will go bad when exposed to air. Should multiple cats with different food requirements live in the household, correct feeding cannot be guaranteed when food is openly accessible. Some cats may have light (or pronounced) eating disorders, i.e. they unlearned to stop eating when they are full. Such cats tend to become obese if food is offered around the clock.

Two meals per day are not appropriate.

(Although some cats will adjust to eating just as much as they need when offered excess food on a regular basis.) Finally, it should not go unmentioned that many cats will get bored and will become too pampered if food is available all the time. Normally your kitty would have to hunt for each meal.

An alternative to free feeding is to serve the cat several meals a day. This option is not perfect either and harbors many risks, particularly when you are dealing with urine-marking cats. Many cats are fed two meals a day – one in the morning and one at night. Unfortunately, this feeding routine is recommended in the majority of cat books. If you keep in mind that outdoor cats will catch and eat between seven and thirteen mice or other small prey in a 24 hour period, it becomes clear at once that just two meals are not natural for cats and that they perceive the waiting time in between two meals to be very long.

If not much is going on in the daytime to keep your cat entertained, feeding times will soon become the (only) highlight of her day. Hunger and anticipation will cause great agitation. A number of cats will show so-called "dry-marking": They assume the same position as for urine-marking, i.e. the tail is erect and trembling, but no urine is released. In such situations, cats who urine-mark frequently will not always stick to dry-marking. If frustration is added to hours of hunger and anticipation of food because the owner is slow to deliver it, another household cat is being served first or claims the shared food dish for herself, or if the food is unacceptable from the cat's point of view, the agitation level can become too high, causing the cat to vent with urine-marking.

- Smells

Smells play a pivotal role in the cat world. Not only do cats leave scents when they urine-mark, but as a matter of fact, they leave scent marks wherever they go. Undetectable for humans, cats leave their own smell with their paws when they walk and especially when they scratch-mark. When they sit down, their anal glands disperse a distinctive smell. Typical is chin rubbing or rubbing of the head's sides against people and furniture, edges, door frames etc. In this way the cat distributes odorous substances (pheromones) produced in different sebaceous glands which help her to create a familiar and peaceful atmosphere in her environment. Also, when your cat rubs against you or a fellow cat with her entire body, she leaves her own scent that will mingle with yours or the other cats' scent. Together, you and your cat(s) create a comforting and intimate group scent. This group scent, as well as her own, gives your kitty a sense of security.

Felines are scent-oriented.

On the other hand, new, strange and obtrusive smells that invade their home territory will strongly upset some cats, and this does not just apply to the scents of a new cat, a newborn child or a new partner. New furniture, new unwashed pillow cases, even a new cat tunnel will cause some cats not just to claim the new item by rubbing their heads against it, but also by urinating on it, integrating it with the help of scent marks.

In households with cats who urine-mark, all objects that carry olfactory greetings from the big wide world into their territory are particularly in danger: shoes, bags and suitcases, but also moving boxes and the wheels of baby carriages.

Another group of potentially hazardous items are those that smell special due to human or animal pheromones. Besides baby clothes, these are especially underwear and any clothing worn directly on the skin, used towels, bath mats and bedding as well as dog beds and blankets. Towels and bath mats are particularly endangered when they have just been used and are still wet.

Sometimes we humans will apply scents to normally familiar and harmless items, causing cats to cover these smells with their urine. Examples are lemon or apple-scented cleaners, fabric softeners with a "spring breeze," detergents that contain ammonia or chlorine, lime-scented glass cleaners – I am sure most of you could supplement this list with your own selection of cleaning products...

- Litter box conditions

In the first part of this book, you already learned what different requirements cats have regarding their litter boxes. Something that is acceptable to one cat may be a far cry from being acceptable to another.

If your cat cannot always feel safe and comfortable in her litter box and therefore is unable to use it, she will suffer great stress. Is the path to the litter box sometimes blocked by a closed door? Is your kitty frequently ambushed on her way to or from the box, or even in it? In all honesty: Do you sometimes forget to remove fresh droppings from the litter box or to clean it regularly? Is it possible that your cat doesn't find her hooded litter box with a swing door as convenient as you?

If one of these aspects applies, it is likely that your cat will urine-mark (more often), possibly combined with typical house-soiling behavior.

Carlo tells his story:

"Basically, there is nothing wrong with my litter box, but often I am glad that I can do my business outside. My human cleans the box about every other day, which is quite disgusting. Rather than using a soiled box, I go outside. Unfortunately a young tom has moved in next door, and he feels that he can claim my territory. Of course he doesn't stand a chance against me, which I am proving to him on a daily basis. I think the marks I leave outside clearly convey the message. Yet sometimes my old bones hurt quite a bit, and I don't feel like fighting every day. Moreover, my favorite elimination spot in the flower bed is right next to the house into which

Less than optimal toilet conditions are a stressor.

he has moved. As soon as he sees me roaming around there, he will dart at me! Of course this drives me mad – how dare he?! If I have to do my business, but can already see him from the window, I am caught between a rock and a hard place. And a full bladder certainly doesn't improve the situation, plus it is next to impossible to fight in such a condition... But I cannot bring myself to use that revolting litter box inside, particularly not when I have already defecated in it. If this dilemma persists for a while, I'll begin to urine-mark the boundaries of my indoor territory to release some of the tension. He never shall dare enter my house!"

Habitual urine-marking

As I emphasized several times, urine-marking is natural cat behavior. It is displayed when the cat is excited, and it is a means of communication.

Urine-marking

If excitement is indeed the reason for your cat's marking behavior, i.e. she marks for a current reason, we speak of "reactive marking behavior." If the reason thereof no longer exists or is removed successfully, no further marking behavior will occur.

Matters will become a bit more complicated if the cat does not mark triggered by a specific situation, but because she is has become used to marking a certain spot over a longer period. This so-called habitual urine-marking behavior can be identified by the

After a while, urine-marking becomes a habit.

fact that the cat doesn't even make an effort to sniff the chosen spot extensively. She will not even turn around to scrutinize the result after marking. A habitually urine-marking cat will briefly stop near the doorframe, couch or chair leg, unceremonially turn her behind toward it, spray and move on.

You probably know from first-hand experience how hard it is to break a habit. Yet it is possible to clearly reduce the frequency or even eliminate urine-marking altogether in a habitually marking cat.

3.3 Solution strategies for urine-marking

Like body language and vocalization, urine-marking is a typical and natural means of communication for cats. For intact males and females of the species, urine-marking is also a means of sexual communication. If you own an unneutered, urine-marking tom or an unspayed cat who marks frequently when she is in heat, please consider neutering or spaying your animal, because there is no therapy that will "cure" normal sexual behavior. There is no one-hundred percent guarantee that neutering and spaying will stop your cat from urine-marking, but chances are high it will stop, particularly if you follow the instructions in the upcoming sections.

There is one rule that applies to all cats, neutered and spayed or not: They must live in our complex human world, while at the same time they have to take care of their "cat business" in their dealings with other felines. Depending on the individual cat's character, it may be easy for them, involve quite an effort, or even be too stressful for them. The latter will sometimes result in urine-marking.

The solution strategies described here serve to identify and reduce the stress in a cat's life by considering her natural needs. Only by taking a "detour" will you be able to reduce the **Urine-marking can be an expression of stress.** occurrence of urine-marking incidents to almost zero. Identifying stressors and eliminating them is not as easy as simply offering one more litter box or cleaning the existing one(s) more often. The measures called for here are a bit more abstract, and the result – a slowly relaxing cat – is much more difficult to observe. This is why I am asking you to take a leap of faith when it comes to taking the steps described for the following methods. Please allow some time for the changes in the cat's environment to take effect and don't expect a completely transformed cat in only a few days. All of the following approaches have been tried and tested, but rarely will urine-marking behavior disappear overnight. Instead, it will decrease in the course of a few weeks.

Cleaning

Please clean the urine-stained surfaces generously and thoroughly with a neutral cleaning agent, alcohol and an enzymatic or anti-bacterial cleaner, because the urine smell invites the cat to mark again (cp. Chapter 2.3, What smells like a litter box...). Make sure you examine vertical surfaces especially carefully, because the puddles on the floor are usually formed by urine that has trickled down a wall or table leg. Wall and table leg must be cleaned as thoroughly as the floor. If you cannot remove all urine traces from the soiled item, you should consider removing it entirely.

Allow your cat access to the cleaned area only after it has completely dried. Your kitty may interpret moist surfaces as an invitation for placing new marks.

To protect your walls until the urine-marking problem has been solved, you can cover them with transparent contact paper or shelf liner at "cat level." There is a risk your cat will try to cover the new smell, but it will be easier to clean the soiled surface. Also, the paper will keep urine from seeping into the walls. If used in time, this measure might save you from having to renovate. Prior to using contact paper, please test it in a hidden place to make sure it can be removed without damaging your walls.

Strategies for cats in the same household

If one or several cats in your household urine-mark, a pivotal solution strategy is to smartly reorganize your rooms and daily routines in order to reestablish peace in your cat community.

Of course each house and each apartment is different. The same applies to the daily routines created by the interaction between humans and cats. As a consequence, I can only suggest rather unspecific strategies that you will have to adapt individually.

Physical structure

Not only the actual floor space of an apartment matters to cats, but the third dimension, i.e. height, is also of importance to them. Cats love elevated places – they enjoy having a full view of everything and feel secure there. In multiple

The third dimension supplies space and comfort.

cat households, elevated places offer also additional space if other felines in residence are perceived to be too close for comfort. Please take a close look at your apartment or house: Can your cats sit on window sills? Can they jump on wardrobes and bookshelves? Have you ever considered building a catwalk under the ceiling made of wood planks or pillars? How about various chairs and armrests, dressers and cabinets? Could you remove some knickknacks to create more attractive spots for your kitties and improve their quality of life in this way?

Such improvements are particularly important in places where passages are no wider than 5 feet (about 1.50 m). Such narrow passages harbor an enormous potential for conflict, especially if tension between cats already exists. If a cat positions herself close to such a passage, she can – while seemingly innocently grooming – block it for other cats. Access to important resources such as the litter box, food, sleeping places, humans or fellow felines is cut off. The victim is not only restricted in her freedom to move, but she might become so agitated that she will urine-mark in the adjacent room.

Does your apartment have narrow passages?

Offering your cats additional space is not just about increasing their quality of life in general, but specifically about peace and a relaxed atmosphere. A shelf on the corridor's wall or sometimes simple items like a chair will allow a cat to cross another one's path without having to get too close.

Resources

A lack of resources can be another trouble spot in a multiple cat household. Are enough warm and cozy sleeping places near the radiator available for all? Does the household have a ceiling-high scratch post with a top view for every cat? Are there enough clean and easily accessible litter boxes? Does your household have a sufficient number of hands to offer pets and cuddles to all kitties desiring them? If all these resources are available in abundance, your cats will have no reason to compete for them, to chase each other away from them, or become agitated about perceived negligence that will lead to urine-marking.

The sufficient supply of desired and (from a cat's point of view) important resources is somewhat complicated by the issue of distance. A window sill that theoretically has enough room for four cats to sit on is not big enough from the perspective of the four cats living together. Imagine a radius of about a bit more than a yard (1 m) around every cat (a length of 2 m with the cat in the middle). This is the so-called individual distance which may only be ignored by particularly well-liked and polite feline members of the household without creating a certain amount of tension. A yard or one meter is only a rough guideline. The individual distance is shorter for some cats and longer for others. Yet most cats appreciate it if this distance is kept. For you, this means that two warm spots next to each other count as one, unless your cats are really best buddies and love to snuggle against each other. Likewise, other elevated resting places as well as scratching devices should be distributed over the entire apartment or house.

Skillfully placed resources help to avoid competition.

Feeding

Feeding is another important process in which humans often ignore cats' individual distance, causing them stress. I am aware that many cats will share the same bowl without fighting, but in many cases these cats would eat slower and enjoy their meals much more if they had their own dishes. Or does one of your cats always wait patiently until another one has finished her meal before she helps herself? This cat would probably be very happy to have her own dish, because she is just as hungry as the one who is already eating. And how can she be sure that there will be any food left for her? Only that much is certain: she will risk a confrontation if she approaches the food too soon – not a very comfortable situation, is it? And you already know what agitation might lead to...

Does each of your cats have her own feeding spot?

Even separate bowls might not be enough. If one or several of your cats eat very fast, check out other cats while eating, assume tense postures or leave immediately when another cat ventures closer, you should consider increasing the distance between feeding spots significantly. Some cats will totally relax only if they are fed alone in a different room. The reason could be that in the wilderness cats hunt alone and do not share their prey. The only exception to this rule is a mother cat supplying food for her offspring.

Play

Hunting brings us directly to the next issue. Especially if your cats are strictly indoor cats, they need variety and occupations to keep them busy and entertained. One of the most important activities of outdoor cats is hunting. If your cat cannot go outside, you must satisfy your

Hunting and play: Recreation for cats.

cat's hunting instinct by playing with her. Your cats don't play? Then it is possible that they don't have the right toys (natural prey animals of cats are usually mouse-sized), or you must improve your play strategy. (Can you imagine a sane mouse jumping up and down under the cat's nose or even *leaping at* the cat?) In a multiple cat household, it may be necessary to separate cats during play sessions. They might not be able to focus on their toy because their play-obsessed buddy constantly pushes them away, or – in the worst case – they must fear attacks from fellow felines as soon as they begin to play. Maybe you will experience a small miracle when you offer your seemingly disinterested kitty a private play session.

I am sure you are aware that sports and physical activities have a calming effect on humans. Jogging through the park after a stressful work day or a dispute can work miracles! Well, keeping your cat occupied and physical exercise according to her needs have a similar effect on her. Tension and pent-up energy along with accompanying agitation will be reduced with constructive results for all parties.

Resting & hiding places

Last but not least, every cat needs the option of retreating and being alone if she wants to. Does your place offer enough open doors, so that your cats can disperse over different rooms? Being alone may indicate that your cat wants to be without another cat. It may also indicate your cat's need to take a "meditative break" from the company of other felines and humans alike.

Retreating has not always to be so thoroughly. Many cats enjoy protected, quiet and cozy sleeping places. Elevated spots warmed by the sun or a radiator where no one disturbs them are in high demand.

Cats need hiding spots from which they can observe their environment.

Your kitty also needs hiding places that allow her to observe without being observed. Such hideaways enable your cat to keep an eye on her ill-tempered feline housemate as well as on the strange new human visitor. If such places for a complete retreat, relaxed sleep or hiding are missing or your cat is constantly being chased away from them, an important pillar of your cat's happiness in life is missing, too – one that provides safety and relaxation.

Strategies for babies, other animals, new persons

It is very useful to think about what it means for your cat if somebody new moves into her territory before it actually happens. Of course, no one is asking you to abandon all your plans for having a family because you hold your cat dear. However, if you share your life with a rather anxious cat, you should think more than twice about getting a dog. A new human partner can be introduced and integrated into your cat's life at a slow pace. In the beginning, limit visiting times and explain your new love what s/he can do to be perceived as polite and non-threatening by your cat. Your new love should avoid direct eye contact with your cat, not try to grab her and actively keep a distance of about one and a half meters (a bit more than 1.5 yards). Leave it to the cat to take the first step toward the new person, but discreet bribes are expressly allowed!

> **Let your cat take the initiative.**

If you are expecting a baby, many changes will take place – from your cat's perspective for worse. Therefore, it is not surprising if she becomes agitated and shows it in a cat's way. To help her cope with the new situation, it is of utmost importance to maintain at least some rituals. Offer your cat something that reminds her of "the good old times" – something she can take comfort in and rely on. Even if it might be difficult, please try to pay the same amount of attention to your cat as before. If you used to play with her in the evening, try to continue to do so. Maybe you'll no longer have half an hour, but at least 10 minutes would be nice. Provide the loving care your cat is accustomed to. Petting her is more than physical relaxation – it is good for her soul.

If you can create positive associations with the child, this is even better than adhering to a certain "standard" of care, and more helpful in avoiding urine-marking behavior. I know, I am asking a lot given this particularly time of your life, but there are many little tricks that take little time and which can greatly help your cat to see the child in a friendly light. Keep a supply of your kitty's favorite food and always have small portions of it handy. Your cat loves chew sticks? Break one into bite-sized pieces and keep it in a small container in your pocket. Be mentally prepared not only to think of your baby, but also of your cat. Now you are all set.

Your cat is entering the room in which you and the child are? Reward her immediately with a friendly word and a piece of her favorite treat. Your cat courageously comes closer to the **Create positive associations.** suspicious baby carriage? Reward her! The baby begins to scream while the cat is in the same room? In this situation, hand out a treat to your cat as fast you can (within a second). In this way, the unpleasant screaming is turned into a signal announcing something good. It will automatically become less threatening. I am aware that realizing this approach takes a lot of effort, but the result is worth it!

So now you are dealing with the cat in a positive way in the child's presence, and you are meeting her need for consistency and routines. Another important aspect is how to deal with smells. Please take out used diapers immediately and throw them in the garbage instead of dumping them in an indoor garbage container first. Don't leave your child's worn clothing lying around, and don't put the child's clothes in a laundry basket from which odors can escape. The intensity of such smells could encourage your cat to urine-mark on clothes and/or in the laundry basket. If you can, use perfume-free products for your child's skin care to avoid the introduction of additional scent sources.

"Good to know that something cool is about to happen ...!"

Strategies for neighborhood cats

The presence of other cats in your neighborhood is a factor pretty much beyond your control. In some instances, you might be able to chase away the aggressive cat from next door in defense of your own kitty, but she will remain a long-term potential threat. In most cases, it is not possible to create a fenced-in, cat-safe environment that also clearly creates a territory border for your own outdoor cat.

Yet there are various things you can do to help your cat to stay calm and relaxed inside your home in spite of the stressful neighborhood – and to keep her from urine-marking.

Please do not invite strange cats into your house, no matter how friendly, pretty or apparently starved they are (if they are really neglected, ask catless neighbors or friends for help or contact local shelters). Also, make sure that strange cats cannot enter your house or apartment. If one of them should manage to enter nevertheless, please expel her immediately! If other cats urine-mark your house, regularly wash the marks away, so your cat doesn't have to smell them.

Since the sight of other cats can lead to immense agitation, it is wise to restrict such visual contact. However, the point is not to keep your cat from being able to look outside and to keep her confined in semidarkness. At times when other cats are very active outside, it is helpful to use window film on the windows' bottom where

Strange cats have no business inside your home.

the view is best. You can buy translucent, yet camouflaging window film with really nice decors at hardware stores. These films can easily be removed later on.

Finally, you can help your cat by decorating your home in such a way that it will be secure and cat-appropriate. Elevated places and observation spots that protect your cat from the view of other cats will make her feel secure. And this is what matters: It is not important that your neighbor's cat actually cannot reach your kitty in your third-floor apartment. Important is only that your cat *feels* safe.

Strategies for hunger, impatience and happy excitement

When you observe that your cat's urine-marking correlates with her feeding times, please try to take the following measures:

Offer exciting activities using dry food.

It is more agreeable with the cat's natural eating pattern to feed her several small portions distributed over the day. If you work in the daytime, start with two small meals – one directly after you got up and the other one shortly before you leave the house. You can serve another portion right after you have come home and another one before you go to bed. An automatic feeder can help in providing another meal during your absence or make sure food is provided in case of an emergency. If you are feeding both wet and dry food, you can stop offering dry food in a dish, which is boring. Put it in toilet and kitchen paper cardboard rolls instead, so that your cat has to make an effort to get it out. Create little hiding places for food in your apartment that your cat will discover accidentally while checking her territory. Later on, she will have to seek out these hiding places frequently. Please keep in mind that in the beginning you will have to make it easy for your cat to find the food. As soon as she succeeds, she will begin to enjoy this task and become better at solving it. Over time, you can slowly increase the level of difficulty.

In many multiple cat households, eating is a hectic affair that goes hand in hand with fighting or threats. Some cats eat extremely fast to keep their even faster companion from stealing their portion. Often they will anxiously look around, anticipating hostile advances in a timely manner in order to clear the battlefield before they are chased away with a paw swat. Others will wait, seemingly patiently, from feeding time beginning to eat what the others have left in the shared dish. All these scenarios are not exactly happy ones for the cats involved and potential sources of stress. After all, eating is about survival!

Please do not feed your cats from the same bowl, but offer them separate small dishes instead. Their eating places should not be too close to each other. The minimum distance between them should be a bit more than one meter (approx. 4 feet). One meter (or a bit more than a yard) is the average individual distance of a cat, i.e. their personal space that they don't like to share unconditionally with other cats or members of other species.

This rule applies also to feeding. If you observe that your cat is unable to relax while eating, raises her head often to check out her environment, lashes her tail, raises her back or tail hair, the distance is not big enough for this cat. In this case, you should increase it to several meters and offer the respective cat an elevated eating place or simply feed your cats in separate rooms. With a little routine, this really doesn't require much effort on your part.

Create daily highlights that don't involve food.

Finally, you can reduce the importance of feeding times somewhat by offering your kitty a diverse and cat-appropriate daily routine with regular play sessions, cuddling time and even intelligent entertainment such as clicker training. With such a daily routine, feeding times will no longer be the only highlight of your cat's day.

Strategies for avoiding strange smells

To give urine-marking cats as little reason as possible for displaying this behavior, you must be careful to avoid strange smells.

Avoid scents known to trigger urine-marking.

If you know that any type of boxlike container will invite your cat to urine-mark, don't leave these standing around for a prolonged time, and certainly not unguarded on your good living room carpet. Always keep in mind that urine-marking is normal cat behavior - you will not succeed in weaning your cat from it. You can only change her level of agitation to the point where she no longer feels the need to mark. However, if the smell of cardboard boxes frequently puts her "in the mood," you must adhere to a strict regime of storing them away.

If your cat loves to pee on shoes, a shoe cabinet is a good investment. Make room for your handbags in a cabinet in the hallway, and store your suitcase away in the basement right after you have returned from a vacation. Don't leave your own and your children's worn clothes out on the floor or on a chair, but put them in a

Do not tempt her!

hamper or laundry basket. If your cat responds to the smells inside these containers, it may help to put the clothes immediately into the washing machine, where they can be locked away almost air-tight. Hang up the towel you have just used higher on the door or drape it over the radiator instead of placing it close to the floor. Your bath mat might also be safer if you dry it on the rim of your bath tub and not on the floor.

From now on, only use cleaning agents with as little perfume and fragrance additives as possible. Everything containing ammonia and chlorine should be banished altogether! As a rule, neutral cleaning agents from various suppliers are the best choice. Also keep in mind that your cat will frequently ingest at least traces of your cleaning agent by licking her paws. This reason might even support your decision to switch to safe and "green" cleaning agents.

However, some problems cannot be solved by avoidance and through strategies for managing them. Of course your dog is entitled to his dog bed, and you, too, are allowed to buy something new for your house, like for example the new shoe cabinet. In this case I recommend you assign a special function to these things that excludes urine-marking (see Chapter 2.3, Strategy # 4: Change the meaning). It can be helpful to let a new piece of furniture air out sufficiently in a cat-safe place after you have unwrapped it. Then proceed to rub the new item with something that carries your cat's scent, for example her sleeping blanket. This will give the new item a more familiar scent.

Strategies for litter box conditions

If you have the slightest suspicion that the type of litter box you own, litter box placement, layout or access to them could be less than perfect, please follow the thorough advice given in Chapter 2.3.

Strategies for habitual urine-marking

If your cat no longer urine-marks for a reason, but because marking has turned into a habit, it does not suffice to change the circumstances that put your cat in an extremely agitated mood

> It's not easy to break habits – this also applies to cats.

and trigger her marking behavior. Besides cleaning the urine-stained spots and removing the initial cause of your cat's distress, you must also break your kitty's urine-marking routines. Changing the meaning of the marked spots is the most important method for achieving this. Since the applicable measures are similar to those taken against typical litter box problems (see Solution Strategies # 2-4 in Chapter 2.3), I will only summarize them briefly here. There are three methods that can help to break your cat's urine-marking habit:

First, remove all urine-marking triggers. If your cat habitually marks your handbag, store all your handbags away.

Second, deny access to all marking spots for an extended period. Put a cabinet in the corner next to the window to cover the spot your cat has frequently used for urine-marking, so this corner will be off limits. Your cat loves to spray the wall while standing on the wardrobe? Make sure she can no longer get up on the wardrobe. Access can also be denied by laying out a material your cat hates to step on. Many cats will avoid various types of films and foils. If you are dealing with a severe case of urine-marking, you may also deny your cat access to an entire room. Always keep in mind not to get carried away, i.e. do not limit your cat's living space too much. Every room and every corner of each room are part of your cat's territory. If all of a sudden you deny her access to a big part of her territory or make major changes to it by putting out shiny aluminum foil everywhere, so that kitty does no longer know where to put down her paws, you will create new stress. Of course this won't help in dealing with a urine-marking cat.

Urine-marking spots can easily be given a new meaning.

Third, give a new meaning to the most heavily used urine-marking spots by changing them into feeding places after you have cleaned them thoroughly. Except for in cases of extreme excitement about food, cats will never mark in close proximity to their feeding places. This is also the cat-friendliest approach, because it does not limit or otherwise affect the cat's territory.

Pheromones

For several years now, artificially manufactured pheromones have been used in cat behavior therapy. They are helpful in supporting other therapy approaches and in helping animals to deal with changes in their environments. Pheromones are messenger substances produced by a creature's body for (chemical/scent-based) communication with members of the same species.

In the context of urine-marking, I recommend Feliway®. Feliway® contains pheromones produced by cats which they distribute in their environment by rubbing their heads against objects and/or humans. Things and people that have been marked in this way will appear familiar to the cat and convey a feeling of safety and comfort. As a rule, items marked with such pheromones will not be marked with urine. The Feliway® diffuser is plugged into an electrical outlet and disperses its pheromone content (odorless to humans) for about a month. One diffuser covers an area of about 50 to 70 square meters (about 540 to 750 square feet).

These pheromones help your cat to feel comfortable and relaxed in her own four walls. You can also purchase Feliway® as a spray that you can apply to typical marking spots after they have been cleaned. Here, too, Feliway® does not deter the cat, but triggers a different response. Instead of marking a certain spot with urine, she will now rub her head against it, given that the area has thoroughly dried off before your cat ventures near.

A pheromone therapy can be valuable in supporting your efforts to cure your cat's urine-marking behavior or rather eradicating the reasons for this behavior, but if pheromones are used alone, i.e. if you don't pay attention to eradicating the actual causes of your cat's marking behavior, you will hardly succeed.

3.4 Urine-marking as expression of an anxiety disorder

Does your cat show other signs of stress or fear as well? Does she often have dilated pupils, even in bright daylight? Does she often lash her tail or raise her hair? Does she frequently throw up her food? Does she tend to retreat, interrupt her sleep or her all-important relaxation periods at the slightest disturbance, always being alert? Is there an ongoing conflict with her companion cats? All these are signs or circumstances that may point to a serious anxiety disorder.

Could your cat's urine-marking indicate an anxiety disorder?

If you can answer any one of the questions with "Yes" and continue to observe these signs after you have taken the measures described in the previous chapters of this book and strictly adhered to them for several weeks, please seek out professional help.

If you can answer more than one of these questions with "Yes" or are not sure, please start applying the methods described here immediately while seeking professional help from a professional cat behavior therapist or from a qualified veterinarian.

During the past years, using Bach flowers, but also homoeopathic remedies, has become a real trend. They are also used to support the curing of behavioral problems. In some cases, they serve this purpose well. In the best interest of your animal, please abstain from experimenting with these remedies, because it is simply not true that they have no side effects just because they are an herbal medicine. Just like any other medication, the responsible and effective application of these cures belongs in the hands of a specialist.

4. Conclusion

You have begun to take the right steps. Instead of helplessly watching your house-soiling cat, you have taken the initiative and gained a better understanding of your cat with the help of this book. I bet you have implemented some of these measures even before you arrived at its final chapter.

This is a good approach, because obtaining theoretical knowledge is just the beginning of your task. In my experience it is best to implement as many measures as possible at once, even if it means a lot of work. If you are taking single steps at a time and don't see results immediately, this does not mean that these steps are ineffective. It just means that they alone are not enough. The right approach is to make further changes. Often success is brought about by making minute changes that all contribute to curing your cat's inappropriate elimination.

Please recall how long your cat has been soiling your house. Two months? Half a year? Three years? How often did it occur? Several times a week? Daily? Even several times per day? All this indicates that your cat must relearn a lot. Some will learn easily and fast as soon as they are offered acceptable conditions. In most cases, progress will be slower or even suffer a few set-backs. In this case, please neither lose your patience nor your optimism. Try to focus on the number of days on which your cat dutifully used her litter box instead of seeing the one mishap.

It is very helpful to keep a diary of your cat's behavior. Buy a little calendar and enter anything related to your cat's inappropriate elimination on a daily basis, i.e. date and time of day of "accidents," their exact location, whether the litter box has been used previously, and which litter box has been used for what "type of business." In any case, please don't forget to enter the days on which your cat did not soil anything. Such a diary will help you to assess your cat's behavior objectively, to notice progress and keep you from overrating mishaps.

If you and your cat succeed, please remain patient and adhere to the changes you made for a longer period. You might even want to adhere to certain aspects of these changes in the future. Give your kitty time to ingrain her new "cleanliness" as deeply and for as long as it has taken her to ingrain her inappropriate behavior. Don't make things difficult for her by hiding the additional litter box away again after just two weeks. You cat needs your help and support, and in her name I would like to thank you for it.

Recommended Reading

Braun, Martina: Chat to your Cat: Lessons in Cat Conversation. Cadmos Publishing Limited, Richmond, 2009.

Dbalý, Helena / Sigl, Stefanie: Playtime for Cats: Activities and Games for Felines. Cadmos Publishing Limited, Richmond, 2009.

Hauschild, Christine: Trick Training for Cats: Smart Fun with the Clicker. Cadmos Publishing Limited, Richmond, 2011.

Heath, Sarah: Why is my Cat doing that? Octopus Publishing, 2009.

Heath, Sarah: Why does my Cat ...? Souvenir Press Ltd, London, 2000 (New Edition).

Morris, Desmond: Catwatching. Three Rivers Press, London, 1993.

Pryor, Karen: Reaching the Animal Mind. Scribner, New York, 2009.

Turner, Dennis C.: The Domestic Cat: The Biology of its Behaviour. Cambridge University Press, Cambridge, 2000 (2nd Edition).

CPSIA information can be obtained at www.ICGtesting.com
Printed in the USA
LVOW102107040613

336947LV00031B/1787/P